INTRODUCTION TO PSYCHOLOGY

HOW TO STOP PROCRASTINATION AND DEVELOP THE SECRETS OF BODY LANGUAGE, REINFORCEMENT, HIDDEN NLP AND VAMPIRISM TO DEVELOP A NEW PSYCHOLOGY OF SUCCESS

Krystal Zhurov

Table of Contents

ABOUT THE BOOK

A person's psyche is as large and sophisticated as the galaxy in which we exist. Your thoughts, nature, and ideas are the products of complex systems that arise in our brains. Psychology is a scientific discipline that tests the mind to interpret actions, sentimental and unconscious states, and a number of other human elements such as interactions and human connections. The Psychology Online Forum helps us learn more about our nature, and by improving our information, men and women can gradually develop as wise beings. One could argue that a widespread version of psychotherapy is any discussion between individuals that is psychologically restful. All the time, people talk to other people, discussing psychologically significant stories from their individual lives. In addition, people constantly look at their own individual characteristics and examine them against the characteristics of other individuals. This type of action is basically diagnostic and is commonly seen in debates of the Psychology Information Forum in general. It's amazing how ordinary men and women are quite innovative and can evaluate details using psychological formulations.

Psychology has many unique subsections. One of these subcategories is the study of developmental psychology. Developmental psychology specializes in the development of an individual's mind throughout a person's life cycle. The online forum for developmental psychology examines the changes that occur in people's thoughts about the world, their feelings, and their behavior in old age. Major milestones in our understanding of the brains of infants and young children have been reached in the past hundred years. These developments have helped various psychiatrists to design concepts related to education and learning and how young children and all of humanity learn knowledge. Many of the current teaching models used in public schools focus on these ideas. The main techniques of psychology, such as investigation, evaluation, and critical thinking, are skills that all men and women have. A number of community psychology online forums are filled with average men and women who do not have official psychology coaching. However, these normal people talk about psychological issues and use critical thinking in an extremely empirical way. This is a simple illustration of many events around the world in which ordinary people show that they use psychological tests to decipher their actions, the people around them, and the important life experiences they experience. The relevance of psychology cannot be underestimated.

Would you believe that NLP techniques can cure your spider phobia in 10 minutes or less? Or that they can nip your smoking addiction in the bud, lift your delay, optimize your golf or bowling performance in record time? Yes, NLP techniques can do these things and more. Let's define NLP first. It stands for neurolinguistics programming. That is the use of language to program the brain. In some ways, it is similar to hypnosis and actually derives many principles and techniques from hypnosis. Both deal with the subliminal or unconscious mind. Hypnosis accomplishes this through trance induction, by putting the consciousness to sleep and dealing directly with the subconscious. NLP uses more sophisticated and covert techniques to bypass awareness. The techniques are known today as NLP has produced some phenomenal results in the areas of therapy, motivation, and performance modeling. NLP practitioners use a variety of powerful NLP techniques such as embedded commands, prerequisites, eye access hints, time distortion, ambiguity, reformulation, deletion, metaphors and parables, and anchoring to achieve some phenomenal results that often seem magical. The exciting thing is that everyone can learn and use many of these techniques to achieve their self-improvement goals and get rid of these self-destructive habits. As an example of using only one technique, we choose anchoring. Let's say you have had traumatic experiences in an elevator ride in the past (perhaps as a child). Now you are very worried and afraid to enter an elevator, maybe even to a full-blown phobia that prevents you from entering an elevator at all. In any case, it would be great to overcome this fear and feel completely comfortable when using the elevator. The trigger mechanism that creates uncomfortable and anxious feelings is likely to be opening the elevator door before entering.

The target here would be to make this incentive a more enjoyable experience. How to do this would be to plunge your head and remember a very pleasant and perhaps fun experience, such as wading on the beach, cycling in the park, or sailing on the lake. If you can vividly remember such an experience and have a warm, safe, out of focus feeling, press your right (or left) earlobe or press your index and middle fingers on your forehead. That is an anchor. In your subconscious, it is associated with the pleasant feelings you experience. You may need to repeat this one or three times to strengthen the connection with the anchor. Now think about it again and imagine that you are standing in front of an elevator door. When the door opens, fire your anchor by squeezing your earlobe or touching your forehead. This will trigger the pleasant feelings you have experienced before. The result will be that your subconscious associates the opening elevator door with the new pleasant rather than the anxious feelings. In fact, you have reprogrammed or rewired your mind to respond differently to the dreaded stimulus, in this case, elevators. Don't be deceived by the clarity of the technology. The subconscious is inherently powerful and highly suggestive. In this way, most traumatic and negative experiences are anchored in our subconscious, and in a split second, a strong stimulus is triggered. These can haunt us for a lifetime if they are not reprogrammed. NLP has all the tools necessary to remove these problematic experiences as quickly as they were stored there.

Stereotypic movement disorder is often associated with intellectual disabilities. It is characterized by repetitive motor behaviors that are not functional, such as: beating the head or swinging the body, causing physical damage, or significantly interfering with normal activities. A child with a short nose, narrow upper lip, small chin, and flat midface, who has developmental delays, failure to thrive, and usually mild to moderate mental retardation, is characterized by non-DSM-related fetal alcohol syndrome (caused by chronic alcohol consumption by the mother during pregnancy). The third leading cause of death in infants between 1 month and one year is Sudden Infant Death Syndrome (SIDS). A child diagnosed with childhood depression may appear similar to a depressed adult, although he often masks his feelings with crime, phobia, under-fulfillment, psychosomatic symptoms, hyperactivity, or aggression. It is often associated with abuse or neglect in the family. The subtypes of personality changes due to a general medical condition are unstable, uninhibited, aggressive, apathetic, paranoid, unspecified, and combined. The most likely diagnosis for a person who becomes catatonic as a direct result of cerebrovascular disease is a catatonic disorder due to a general medical condition. Substance poisoning is diagnosed if changes in behavior or psychological changes occur during or shortly after use or exposure to a substance (e.g., alcohol, caffeine, opioids), and the changes are due to the substance's physiological effects on the central nervous system.

Substance deprivation occurs when a person develops a reversible syndrome because the use of a substance has recently been discontinued or reduced after being used in large quantities for a long time. A customer who has reported extensive use of LSD in the past, but is no longer used, reports that he occasionally experiences hallucinations that are similar to what he experienced using LSD. In this case, the most appropriate diagnosis is hallucinogen persisting perception disorder. A person with delirium suffers from a reduced awareness and understanding of the environment, a reduced ability to concentrate, to maintain or change attention (impaired consciousness) as well as from memory problems, disorientation, or language difficulties (cognitive disorders). Sometimes illusions or hallucinations (perceptual disorders) occur instead of cognitive disorders.

The three storage levels are sensory memory, short-term/primary memory, and long-term / secondary memory. The sensory offers short storage of information after the stimuli have been removed. The information remains available for no longer than 2-3 seconds. The ability to temporarily remember multiple facts or thoughts while solving a problem or performing a task is related to working memory. The articulation loop refers to the process of quickly repeating the information to be remembered verbally in order to facilitate its retention in the working memory. One way to believe that information gets into long-term memory is to do a thorough rehearsal or think about the meaning of new information and its relationship to the information that is already in memory. Information that has been stored in long-term memory is retained there permanently unless the brain is impaired due to an illness or substance use. Explicit (declarative) memory is the deliberate reminder of past experiences and information (e.g., remembering appointments), while implicit memory refers to when previous experiences help to perform a task without consciousness (e.g., conditioned answers).

When a person is asked to remember a list of unrelated words, research has shown that they tend to remember words best from the beginning (primacy) to the end (actuality) of the list. This is known as the series position effect. Flashbulb memory refers to vivid memories that arise in minimum detail from personally meaningful and emotionally charged events. Research has shown that flash memories fade with time. People with anterograde amnesia have a normal recall of previously learned information but cannot save newly learned information, while people with retrograde amnesia are able to store and retrieve new information but cannot retrieve previously learned information. Loci's method is to first link memorabilia to visual images, then mentally place the images in a familiar space, and finally, mentally walk through the space to remember the objects. The ability to keep a mental snapshot of an object even after it is removed is known as Eidetic Imagery (also known as photographic memory). The coding specificity hypothesis (also known as state-dependent memory) states that a person can retrieve information better if the relationship between coding, storage, and retrieval is closer. Contextual dependence refers to the fact that information retrieval is better when the learning and retrieval environments are the same, while state dependency refers to the fact that information retrieval is better when the emotions during learning and retrieval are similar. When a new experience disrupts the recall of an earlier memory, it is called a retroactive disorder, while proactive disorder occurs when previously learned information disrupts the newer learning.

SPIRITUALITY IN PSYCHOLOGY

The field of psychology includes many aspects that have to be dealt with every day. Therapists and others working in the field are often faced with moral dilemmas that can lead them to question the place of morality and spirituality in psychology. Those who practice any form of religion can use their specific values and morals to find solutions in these situations. The question remains whether religion has a place in the daily practice of psychology and, if so, where the line can be drawn. In part, psychology is viewed as a science. While not accurate in all situations, it has several similarities to science when it comes to theories and decisions. Ethics play an important role in psychology, both for the psychologist who performs the evaluations and the treatment and for the client or patient who receives the services or the treatment. The Code of Ethics was introduced to protect both parties. Morals are based on right and wrong and can, therefore, in many cases, be closely related to morality. For this cause, it can be argued that religion plays a role in the ethical decisions that are made every day. Although the Code of morals does not specifically state religion as part of what it contains, there are various aspects of morality and shared values. Spirituality, as a whole, has become widespread in the field of psychology in recent years, as evidenced by the number of Christian advice centers that have opened across the country. The professionals who work in these environments offer an excellent combination of treatment, psychology based on Christian values and beliefs. Here, the psychological principles and ethics are used with various aspects of religious values and beliefs that are woven into the treatment plans. Patients are often advised on how spirituality can help them in their difficult situations. In these situations, professionals strive to strike a balance between psychology and religion, which is sometimes a challenging task. Psychology is based on diverse principles, theories, and ethics, while religion is mainly based on belief. Psychological problems are scientifically proven, while much of religion is based on a belief in the invisible. While many people do not question their beliefs, it can be difficult to mix what can be seen physically with what cannot. As a result, many people question the place of spirituality in psychology. Because belief is often questioned, it has become necessary to get evidence. This witness often comes in the form of responses that directly result from the testing of opinions (Myers). When opinions are tested and found to be correct, it is easier to maintain faith. However, if they fail the test, belief can become a very uncertain perspective. If this principle is applied to psychology, the result can change regularly.

Different situations require different ideas that may or may not be effective. What works in one situation can also prove impossible in another. The key to understanding where spirituality fits is knowing how to apply it to every situation and idea and making determinations and judgments based on the information gathered and the specific values that are relevant to the end result. To better discern where religion fits into the psychological realm, let's take a closer look at the human characteristics that make up each. When it comes to religion, there is theological wisdom. This is about accepting divine love to enable the individual to accept himself. However, psychological wisdom deals with self-respect, optimism, and personal control (Myers). The ability to use both together to make important decisions gives us the freedom to use what we know, to admit what we don't know, and to look for answers. Because we are both creatures and creators of our social world, people and situations are important (Myers). While final control lies with us, we are responsible for making important decisions that have a lasting impact on us and others. Psychologists face these dilemmas every day. They have to make important decisions that directly affect their patients. Each decision is made individually and depends on the particular situation and circumstances. Each decision will involve a separate set of ethical questions and dilemmas, and the solution will remain unique to each decision. Religion is supposed to heal people, while medicine is supposed to do the same. The two often work in different contexts, but it can be argued that medicine was discovered based on ideas and values based on religious beliefs. For this reason, it is believed that in many situations, both are used together to create treatment plans that are both effective and long-lasting.

In many ways, people who have faith have discovered the insights and critical analysis of psychology helpful in understanding human nature. Your assumption that religion promotes happiness and health is also largely attributed to psychology. The science of psychology provides principles that can be applied to constructing messages that are memorable and convincing. Here the tasks of peacebuilding and reconciliation are promoted in such a way that solutions are offered with which others can be happy by building healthy relationships. While science can question our way of thinking, the same can be said of religion. Faith is often questioned to find answers. This has proven useful in many situations where the answer was not clearly defined. Here the science of psychology, along with religious beliefs, is used to find solutions to problems that seem to have no immediate or clear solution. However, belief is not always a negative aspect of psychology. A strong system of values and beliefs can help a psychologist who works as a specialist in the field copes with situations in which traditional psychological theories do not provide a clear answer. In this case, the process is reversed because religion is used to clarify certain circumstances based on the absence of information that can be gathered at a particular time. There are also times when one can support the other. Religious beliefs are used to support the reasoning behind many ethical situations, while psychology is often used to demonstrate different religious ideas. Here the two can be used together to find a truly unique solution that works.

It has also been argued that belief plays an important role in a psychologist's ability to use the information contained in the Code of Ethics and Psychological Practices that is available every day. This is based on the conviction that people with strong faith understand the science of psychology better because they can use both together to find answers that are appropriate for each new situation. Here, psychologists neither rely on faith nor science but use both of them to understand the situation as a whole better. Those who believe in the content of the Code of Ethics understand its meaning and why they have to play a role in psychology every day. Those who have a strong religious belief usually strive to use it every day when making ethical decisions and often strive for a result that is based on both science and belief. Still, there is a crucial line between using psychology and relying on beliefs and values that often help many make decisions in everyday life. When it comes to mixing psychology and spirituality, everyone has their own place. The scientific aspects of psychology are necessary to solve a variety of problems and successfully treat those in need. Nevertheless, spirituality can play a very important role in the rehabilitation of patients by facilitating the understanding of the psychological effects and the reasons for their existence. Spirituality and science can be applied both during and after treatment. During treatment, religious beliefs can lead both the psychologist and the patient to make the right decisions and understand difficult situations along the way. After the treatment, religion can help the patient in his/her further life, while the scientific aspect remains in the form of constant advice or medication.

Psychologists can use both in their vocation to make difficult decisions and deal with difficult-to-solve problems. You can rely on each aspect to draw important conclusions that can be helpful throughout the treatment process. It has also been shown that psychologists who know their profession but also have a strong religious belief can help their patients throughout the treatment by passing on various virtues that promote positive thinking. The end results of the fusion of science and spirituality have been explored for a few years. Some argue that psychology should only remain a science, while others believe that the intertwining of science and religion can only help improve treatment situations' overall outcome. It is also argued that science as a whole is closely related to religion and that the two often give reason to question one another. Science could often prove what religion can't, and religion was the basis for the need to know, and so people began to investigate the how and why of scientific matters and how to relate to others. One point is the association of scientific ideas presented in daily human nature with religion and the ability to place the information to show how it all relates. Another important point is the connection between religion, prejudice, altruism, and general well-being. When dealing with different psychological situations, it is just as important to recognize the importance of science as religion is. This is often difficult because the individual specialists in this area represent different beliefs and values. For this reason, it is necessary for everyone to make decisions based on the psychological code of ethics, together with the specific circumstances of the situation. For those who are religious, spirituality will play the biggest role in decision making in a professional setting because it is very likely to be the case with everyone else. Those who use spirituality in everyday situations rely on leading them in their professions. Although the psychological code of ethics may not have been specifically created based on religious beliefs and values that are directly related to spirituality, there are many similarities between ethical dilemmas and intentions and those of a moral nature.

Relationships between belief and subjective well-being have also been reported. Even if the science of psychology and spirituality should be brought together in a professional setting can be somewhat subjective, as it depends on the different situations and those who are straight involved in the treatment processes. While they are linked between the ethical code that psychologists apply everywhere and the morality combined with religion, the two remain independent. They can be used in any given situation where they are considered necessary or important. The code of ethics is applied every day in the psychological environment, but whether or not spirituality is involved can be left to any professional working in the field.

MINDSET: THE NEW PSYCHOLOGY OF SUCCESS

The potential of positive thinking has been a topic of discussion for years. Why should they call the mindset "new psychology of success"? The theory of professing to be a success is not new, as Wallace Wattles wrote "The Science of Getting Rich." But how much of the stuff from a hundred years ago are we following today? Strange that more and more evidence spawned this old man's theories 100 years ago. We still find more things today to prove the theory right and not wrong. Now, what is the new psychology of success? Physicists have found that positive and negative frequencies attract or push away exactly what we want. What decides most about what frequency you are on is your emotional state. Think about your life and everything in it. Physicists tell us that at a certain level, you have created everything in your life. We can transform our lives based on this new success in psychology. But what about the new psychology of success to create financial freedom? Don't we all want that? So why doesn't this new success psychology always work for everyone? Here's the catch: It's not really "positive thinking"; It is a "positive feeling." And, let's face it, it's pretty difficult to be in control of your emotions all the time. So it takes practice, and therefore the change of mindset does not happen overnight. You have to pay attention to your feelings. For example, you may be attending a training webinar to make money online and find that the majority of callers make over $ 10,000 a month. So you think, "Why can't I make that much money?" "What's wrong with me?" NOT CORRECT!! You think about what could be wrong with you! You must not compare yourself to others; you can continue to look forward to what you have become and thank you for the special person you are. Special person? Yes, think about it. You have performed certain things in your life that many others have not. You have people in your life who you love and who would be lost without you. Give yourself credit where it's due, and feel grateful for the accomplishments in your life! (Gratitude emotion is the highest frequency besides love. So if you really feel grateful, you will probably attract your desires.) But here's a little exercise to help you lift your emotions. Write a letter explaining what is good about you. The more things you think about, the more things will come to mind. We often don't like to brag about ourselves, so these thoughts are suppressed in our angles, and we don't honor ourselves. For each achievement or trait, you write about yourself, add "thank you" to the end of each statement. Gratitude creates blessings - and that's the new psychology of success! Fact: Albert Einstein has tried hundreds of times every day to say thank you for the tools, ideas, and fellow scientists in his life and to see what great things he did! So how can you adapt to the new psychology of success?

Do you remember a time when you were up there in the world? The people around you or the person you were with were completely and deeply inspired by your actions and words. Close your eyes and remember this time and feel the sensations you had at that time ... relive the experience. Now rewind and run again. Once you have arrived at a point where you can activate these feelings like a light switch, imagine that you would feel these feelings in your future situation that you want to achieve. The high energy frequency you feel attracts your deepest desires. So what can you do now? Offer free service for people who want to change their mindset for success. It can also help you to know real exams that successful people have had to overcome. What is success for you? Success is different for everyone. Everyone wants to be successful in various things, be it in their careers or in their studies. Success is basically about achieving the goals you set yourself. If you want to achieve the goals you set yourself to be successful, you need to have a certain attitude. Of course, the way things develop also plays a big role in your success. However, the state of mind is the most important factor for your success. This mental state of success is the psychology of success. You need to have four key personality traits that can help you become successful. First, you have to learn to make your own decisions. You should not be pushed into other decisions by people, or your decisions should not change due to the circumstances. When you have made a decision, you should be determined to stick to that decision. This will take you one step closer to the goal you set, instead of turning to a completely different goal and leaving the first goal behind. You also need to be sure and be able to control your mindset. The way you think determines your view of the outside world. If you think negatively, you will see all opportunities with a negative perspective and may not even attempt to achieve your goal. However, if you think positively, you can win success for yourself. This is another part of the psychology of success. Control how your mind thinks and how you control it to achieve your goals.

Your attitude toward success is very important. With the wrong attitude, it is very unlikely that you can achieve your goals. The right mindset has a huge impact on your determination and the way you do things to achieve your goals. With a constructive attitude, you will work more enthusiastically and with greater determination to achieve your goals, and you will do so successfully. The psychology of success also says that you have to have the right character to be successful. There is a certain quality that successful people have, such as commitment, positivity, competence, etc. If you feel that you lack these traits, you need to build on them to be successful. The psychology of success also says that you also have to have values. If you think something is honorable or dishonorable, stick with it and don't falter. That's the most important; not to deviate from your values because that changes the direction of your goal and your success. Success psychology also believes that you should know your goals on hand. Don't just wander aimlessly and hope to succeed. The psychology of success is made very simple. Your mental state plays a crucial role in setting and achieving goals!

How to initiate the psychology of success

Creating a positive awareness of success is the only permanent means of achieving a good, rewarding lifestyle. The psychology of success has to be proficient and implemented again and again. Every successful individual trusts in the power of positive confirmation when starting campaigns or rather working towards targeted goals. To trigger such thoughts, one should be able to notice and rely on the power of the mind. There is no restriction on what a focused mind can achieve. The mind is shaped to attract or repel success. Anyone who is aware of the psychology of success confirms the fact that the universal laws of attraction go hand in hand with the types of thoughts that we stimulate in our heads. For example, a person who allows negative thoughts to suppress his mind is doomed to fail in everything he does. A negative attitude before doing an activity becomes a recipe for failure. On the other hand, people who have been trained to influence positive affirmations are successful in any activity they choose. To be successful, they have to rely on their inner abilities. They should be able to detest negative thoughts and stimulate thoughts that make them achieve what they want. Visualization is one way to generate a positive mind. Positive mental images created for your desired goal promote positive affirmations that create a lifestyle geared toward that goal. An individual who is interested in financial freedom will stimulate thoughts about financial freedom in their thoughts. Detailed thoughts can be those who live in expensive houses, drive expensive cars, and most likely run a multi-billion dollar business empire. Such thoughts are the epitome of financial freedom. If you believe in your mind, you have what it takes to achieve what you want; then, this individual will surely get there. It is limited to understand that the results may not be visible overnight and that it can sometimes take years for them to arrive. However, an individual should always find strength in the fact that every day is a step towards the desired success. A prepared mental attitude to achieve successful psychology is the most important aspect for every person who might be interested in achieving this self-development goal. It is very easy for the mind to create positive affirmation from information with which it can relate.

Education is a major factor if you want to achieve your goals. Education eliminates ignorance and helps not only to grow intellectually but also in terms of leadership, experience, personal development, and environmental knowledge. You acquire skills that you would not otherwise have had, and you can think creatively. It is difficult to achieve your goals if you are not in good health. You have to be healthy, physically and mentally. Physical health can be achieved through a balanced diet, exercise, lots of sleep, cleanliness, and good excretion. Mental health can be achieved through positive thinking and an appropriate mindset. To be successful, you have to be determined and self-determined. Passion gives you the energy to be focused and achieve your goals. These principles make you successful in every aspect of life. If you assume that you are rich or climb the career ladder, you have to observe the psychology of success. Individuals who are determined to succeed but failed usually lack one or more of these factors that are critical to achieving their goals. Most people lack focus because they have no fixed goal. You don't have to look at other lucrative things or easier to achieve because you lose focus just to realize that they are lost and discouraged. To become famous, you have to be outstanding regardless of the obstacles and hurdles along the way.

REVERSE PSYCHOLOGY

Reverse psychology is a crazy technique to give someone the impression you want a certain result if you actually want the opposite. It makes you influence other thoughts to make a change without being direct, so you remain responsible for making that change. Used positively or negatively, this is a kind of manipulation of a person's thought pattern that completes a predicted change with the result that there is no visible influence. It is also defined as telling someone something that is the opposite of what they are supposed to do or believe. Reverse psychology can be used in relationships. Men generally complain that women always say the opposite of what they think. Maybe women are only programmed to be reverse psychologists? If you think your partner is continually saying the opposite of what she feels, you can try to use the same concept to your advantage. At work, reverse psychology can lead to the corner office, salary increases, or even promotion. This is particularly useful when you are in sales. You can apply it to your customers and clients. The idea is primarily to get your customers interested right away, believing that they really need your product or service. That her life is just not complete without her. When you use this technique to give your customers the impression that your loss is their benefit or that you have much more to lose than they, they suddenly feel like you are doing them a favor, and they are much more eager to do so close a deal, this technique can increase productivity and sales. As a parent, it is common knowledge that children are notorious for waiting for you to tell them something and then doing the opposite. Nobody knows why, but children live by doing the opposite of what is expected of them. This can be a version of reverse psychology in and of itself! So, as a brilliant parent, you are trying to put your own reverse psychology into practice. By telling your children the inverse of what they should do, they can exactly do what you want them to do. However, it is vital to remember that children are small beings that can be influenced. Use reverse psychology only in special circumstances and avoid using it in a way that could affect your child's understanding of self-esteem.

What and when is the perfect way to apply reverse psychology to your children? Don't use reverse psychology as your first choice. Use sparingly if all other methods fail. Use a positive form instead of a negative one. While this can encourage a child to learn harder, it is just as likely that the child will believe and give up on you. And that feeling can last a lifetime. Offer your child a choice so that it feels independent. For example, if he/ she refuses to take a bath, say, "OK. So when the bath time is over, it's time for bed. Challenge your child instead of giving orders. For example, say, "I bet I can finish my vegetables before you finish them. Use a positive reward system. For example, make a "Prize Jar" for each child and enter a coin when they complete a task or behave correctly. Distribute the prize money regularly (daily, weekly, etc.). Avoid competition between siblings. Stay calm and do not react emotionally if your children are misbehaving or persistent. Losing coolness creates the conditions for a situation without profit. People against whom reverse psychology can be used effectively are narcissists, people who actually only think about themselves. When they think about themselves, they are isolated from society and the world, and their lives become entangled in an environment where there is only loneliness. They are deprived of love, take care that they actually have to get, and this, in turn, causes them to lose their trust.

Reverse psychology can be used effectively against these people because they are easily aroused and tend to work in opposite ways. The people who are high-spirited: These types of people have so much self-confidence that they think that they are always the best, and whatever they do is accurate. They find it useless to accept suggestions and advice from others. Such people are actually intelligent fools, and if you use the technique of reverse psychology, you can easily use them to your advantage. A persistent person is a person who does not change their ideas or thoughts towards another person and tries to prove themselves and correct them all the time. Reverse psychology can be used against these types of people because they think they are right and the rest of the world wrong. If you want a stubborn person to do your job, you can do so by supporting their perspective and using them to get your job done. The people who have less willpower get nervous easily, and they totally believe in what they are told. They take advice from many people before approaching a decision. In this contrast, they become confused and make wrong decisions. They can also be used by reverse psychology. Among self-confident people, there are people who are negative about certain things and who also lack self-confidence. These types of people are easily prone to reverse psychology.

How do you use reverse psychology?

Be aware of the person; every person does not respond to reverse psychology. Before using this technique on another person, you need to be aware of the type of person against whom you are using the reverse psychology technique. Wait for the right circumstance; reverse psychology is most useful when the person is in an over-excited or emotional state. Contrary to what you actually argue, be ready to take action, and never threaten anyone unless you believe you can take effective action against them. Since reverse psychology is an approach related to the use of the brain and psychology, it must be used with extreme caution; otherwise, it can also negatively affect. The technique of reverse psychology should be applied against the right person. When used against the wrong person, it can be extremely harmful. Excessive use of reverse psychology can be harmful because the other person may learn that you are using reverse psychology against them. In such a situation, the person would begin to influence the opposite of what is real. Reverse psychology, when used appropriately, can be widely used in daily life, with vital and widespread reverse psychology is largely beneficial to human society.

THE DISEASE CALLED PROCRASTINATION

You were given a task. The deadline is approaching. But you don't have the energy to do it, no eagerness to work on it. You think it can be done later, tomorrow, or even another day. This is called deferral. It is the process of delaying an essential task and focusing on a less important, simple, and entertaining task. You postpone a task until the "last minute." Postponement is a habit that has, in some ways, negatively affected many people. It's actually painful and shameful to put it off. You do not feel well. Your body is not as usual. They promise that it will only pass. That you'll be fine. Something more is developing. Something bad. Your health has deteriorated. You now decide to see a doctor. The doctor tells you it looks impossible because your problem has become inoperable. If you had come earlier, your problem could have been resolved. The problem is that you hesitate. Reluctance is a habit that can become a bitter enemy for you. It brings nothing but stress, disappointment, and fear. As much as we should believe that postponement is bad - that makes us lazy, unreliable, and unprofessional, it also has advantages. Some people will deliberately delay work because they love working under pressure. Delay actually has some advantages. The positive side of the postponement is that it gives individuals time to tackle troublesome problems and develop more ideas. You'll have time to pay bills, attend meetings, get involved in other projects, and then you'll have plenty of time to do what you're supposed to do. It cannot be denied that there are really inevitable cases where the individual has to adopt the postponement habit. This leads to creativity. If you get a task that is so difficult for you, hesitate to do it better. You may have a better and more consensual idea of getting the job done because you've given yourself enough time to think about it. This leads to better decision making.

Postponing gives an individual time to think and gather more information, which leads to a better selection. Unnecessary work can be eliminated if you hesitate. When you get a task, you are delayed, and unwanted, non-essential work may be dropped when an important task arrives. This task, which you do not like, will be for a short time in your life, as you have done for a short time. However, over time, postponing it becomes a habit in your life. You have no choice but to stop it. If you don't stop it on time, it will destroy you. The postponement has so many disadvantages, including ruining your postponement prevents you from going over your deadline and reaching your goals. This can have serious ramifications for your career, as you may miss a promotion or even lose a job. Damage your reputation - you promise to do something. You do not do this. This affects your image because nobody loves vague promises. Apart from that, you are also killing your self-confidence and self-esteem, as it is nothing new for you if you hesitate. People will not have hope for you and may not give you chances because they fear that you will be disappointed. If you hesitate, you will not feel well. You become stressed, anxious, and depressed. This leads to health problems. You can't achieve your goals - people set goals because they want to achieve them and maybe want to make a change in their lives. If your goals are distracted by postponement, you are also distracting your future life. If you take advantage of opportunities - deferment will waste opportunities that would otherwise have changed your life. Opportunities, as they say, come only once. If the world gives you one, avoid the delay, and seize this opportunity! Wasted time cannot be restored. Delay is a good time-eater! You will regret not having used it for a certain period of time. Your precious time has passed, frustration creeps in, and you know you could have done something, but you haven't done anything.

PROCRASTINATION PROBLEM

What are some of the causes of postponement? There are two that stand out as the main cause of the delay: perfectionism and impulsiveness. The ideas behind these two possible causes are clearly not able to start or end a task because the result never meets the perfectionist's unrealistic standards. For the impulsive person, the delay is the result of an inability to crumple and really concentrate on one thing. It is the theory of the "shiny object" of postponement. The impetuous procrastinator may have too many projects at once or create new ones in order not to do the perhaps more unpleasant work. How well do "perfectionism" and "impulsiveness" explain the phenomenon of procrastination? Let's start with perfectionism. Does perfectionism postpone? Certainly, to different degrees, it affects some people more than others. Of course, this leads directly to the problem with this theory: Not everyone is a perfectionist. Nevertheless, everyone hesitates to a certain extent. The source of procrastination is unlikely to be rooted in a psychological trait, such as perfectionism or impulsiveness. It would be nice to be able to spot a specific cause, but it's just not that easy. No, deferral is not "caused" by anything. It is part of who and what we are. It is an inherent characteristic of humanity. The heart of the delay is our actual evolution as a species. That would explain why hesitation affects everyone. You see, people weren't focused on long-term planning; two different "types" of postponement: simple and chronic. Simply postponing is the way you are simply not inclined to do something because it is boring or uncomfortable. This can be reasonably explained by inadequate impulse control or perfectionism or the inability to engage in long-term planning. A simple postponement can be overcome in several ways. What about chronic postponement? For example, are you hesitant to file taxes for years, or are you unable to complete a relatively undisputed hardware store project for an entire summer? This kind of hesitation takes months or years and can even ruin lives. It is omnipresent and a source of significant stress. And it resists most attempts to overcome it. The essence of chronic postponement is the feeling of being "disturbed" or some kind of low-level fear. This feeling arises whether you are aware of it or not - and whether it makes sense at all to feel that way. In other words, the chronic deferral object, such as overdue taxes or an incomplete project, is considered a major threat and triggers a deep drive to avoid this. Chronic delay can be the result of a perceived existential threat. That is, the mind literally has to do with whatever it is, with the possible death as a result.

Does the mind actually relate something generally unpleasant, such as the final settlement of overdue taxes, to death? What some consider uncomfortable is seen by others as a disaster. For example, some people would prefer to give a speech to a live audience. Something almost as bad as death (as far as the brain is concerned) has proven to be profoundly wrong. Not just wrong, but deeply wrong or grossly incompetent. Have you ever felt that way? That you would do anything not to endure the ridiculousness of your colleagues? Chronic delay and total avoidance seem like a similar kind of fear. Somehow, the brain has associated the object of chronic deferral - in the example above, overdue taxes - with a massive punishment. Indeed, there is a massive penalty that could result directly from the non-payment of taxes. So why does the tax avoider make the situation worse by not addressing the problem at all? There is no reasonable explanation for chronic postponement any more than there is any reasonable explanation for depression or anxiety. The person concerned may feel that there is nothing they can do. They have become powerless or helpless to make significant progress. It is pure motivational paralysis - a feeling of deep inner conflict and sometimes the inability to recognize the problem at all.

The definition of procrastination, were you born this way?

Postponement is the habit of postponing an action or task much later. This word comes from the Latin pro and means "forward, forward or in favor" and crostini, which means "of tomorrow." Delay is considered by many to be a negative attitude, a counterproductive habit. But it is seldom seen positively as a functional delay or avoidance of haste. In addition, each common idea only reveals a core or essential element. It is obvious that all deferment definitions and conceptualizations indicate that a task or decision must be postponed, delayed to match the Latin origin of the word. Based on this, a procrastinator is someone who delays starting or completing an action or task. This distinction is relevant because there are hundreds of tasks that can be done at any time, and it becomes tedious to think that you will postpone all of them. Delay is particularly common nowadays. Everyone seems to be affected. It is like a modern illness that knows no race, gender, age, or limit. Some of us may have postponed tasks from time to time, but for some, it is a way of life for them. So why are so many people hesitating? Are we born this way? The answer is a big NO. We become conditioned procrastinators. One of the purposes is that we are not investigating what leads to delays. Those who want to stop the deferral must first identify the main causes only if you know why you can make the changes to overcome the delay. Fortunately, a specific physiological analysis of the postponement has been done, and when everything is said and done.

The dictionary definition of postponement is the process of postponing, delaying, or postponing, especially out of habitual negligence or laziness. Delay basically means that actions with high priority are replaced by tasks with low priority, and important tasks are postponed to a later point in time. A procrastinator has to deal with the question of why the task is postponed. The identifying reason alone will be the motivating force to take action and perform the erroneous task. Postponement is essentially a thief of time. Time management experts can say write a "to-do list" and check it. You can tick things and still avoid what was really important because obviously, it can go on the list from tomorrow. But when a new day begins tomorrow, other things always seem to have priority. Procrastinators are not born that way. They arise over time. The kidnapping habit can be learned in the family and in the school of life. It's more of a learned act, by subjecting yourself to pressure or fear of failure. Learned behavior can be forgotten so that procrastinators can change - step by step. Why don't we attach importance to very important tasks? Believe that procrastinators tell themselves lies or not. They don't see themselves in their true light; they say things like, "I feel more like doing this tomorrow." Or "I will work best after I have slept well." But in reality, they don't get an urge the next day and work best after a break. They also justify themselves that "that is not really that important." Procrastinators can actually waste their resources. There are many ways to sabotage your success yourself, and deferment is the choice of the path that people take without realizing that they are. Hesitant behavior can be a measure to avoid the fear of failure or even success. Some procrastinators are very concerned about what others think about them. They prefer to make others think that they lack effort rather than skill. By not making decisions, procrastinators release themselves from responsibility for the outcome of events.

Postponing them can be expensive. Health is one and productive life. Deferment can lead to feelings of guilt, stress, and insomnia, which in turn can lead to a strong loss of personal productivity and a strain on personal relationships. It tends to shift the burden of responsibility onto others who may get angry. It is, therefore, very important to change or reduce this behavior. You can change this predominant and self-sabotaging behavior. Perfectionism, a tendency to negatively evaluate results and one's own performance. Intense fear and avoidance of others' assessment of their own abilities. You increased social self-confidence and fear. A repeated bad mood like finding out why you're hesitating is the first step toward transformation. For example, there can be many reasons;

Fear, aversion, pressure, boredom, and avoiding responsibility. This habit has evolved over a long period, so that the change will take time. You can change your behavior. Just don't expect to change it overnight. You can experiment with different strategies because the same strategy doesn't work for everyone.

Types of procrastinators

There are basically two types of traffickers: one tense and one relaxed. The tense guy often feels both a strong pressure to succeed and the fear of failure. The relaxed guy often feels negative about work and blows it off - forgets it - by playing. The rejection-based type of procrastinator avoids as much stress as possible by dismissing work or ignoring more challenging tasks and focusing on having fun or doing other distracting activities. The type of procrastination with fear of tension is described as overwhelming, unrealistic about the time, uncertain about the goals, dissatisfied with the success, undecided, accused of others or circumstances of failure, lack of trust, and sometimes also perfectionist. The underlying fears are, therefore, failure, lack of skills, imperfection, and falling short of overly demanding goals. This guy believes that his worth depends on what he does, which reflects his abilities. He/she is scared of being judged and found defective. In this way, this type of procrastinator is overwhelmed and reworked until he temporarily escapes the pressure by relaxing, but every enjoyment gives rise to guilt and greater concern. Therefore procrastinators are classified as: Perfectionists - who are afraid to do something less than good idealists - who have great ideas but hate to do the details everything that other crisis makers are expected to do - who do it in Finding any bidder (often by starting too late) or making it a big problem - who take on too many tasks. If you hesitate, you must end the hesitation problems before they have a profound negative impact on your life. A procrastinator often fights because he or she postpones things. Some procrastinators find that they procrastinate only in one area of their life, such as work, while others procrastinate that they delay necessary tasks in all areas of their lives. In any case, hesitation can cause problems and should be stopped. Delaying can be so deeply rooted for some people that they don't even know they are doing it, and that makes stopping difficult. Deferment treatment is available, however, and can help people stop this bad habit. Effective anti-procrastination techniques include NLP and hypnotherapy.

How to stop the procrastination problem?

Most people are faced with the question of how to stop the delay and start doing tasks. The decision to end the delay is up to the individual. Once the decision is made, drawing up a successful plan is very important. Adherence to the plan is also important to stop the delay. Some practical steps have to be followed while the problems of postponement are rooted out. Once the answer to the question of how to stop the delay is found, the entire life pattern of individuals will change permanently. The answer increases the true potential of the individual and enables new motivation, commitment, and energy in solving the problems with which the life span is confronted. There are various reasons for people's abduction habits. These reasons range from fear of success or failure or just laziness. By determining the reasons for the postponement, a suitable plan for its eradication can be developed. This plan must focus on how to stop the delay. The plan will help people get motivated and give them a better life. Confidence is the main factor for motivation. Fear of rejection, fear of failure, and the feeling of being unworthy are the most common reasons for the delay. Taking positive steps in building self-confidence increases the chance of being motivated. The delay in itself is a reason for the lack of self-confidence of the individuals. This leads to stress, fear, and guilt feelings that lead to unfulfilled dreams and goals. This increases the need to discover the methods by which the delay can be stopped.

Pain and pleasure are the two most important things that motivate people in particular. To list the joys that can be expected from reaching the goals set, it is necessary. In addition, the disadvantages of the postponement must be listed in relation to the goals set. A certain level of soul searching and evaluation of individual life is very important. Overcoming irrational fears and phobias, disregarding rewards, and focus help stop the delay. These are important steps to strengthen the self-confidence of the individual. If individuals do not like each other for lack of courage to pursue their goals, then they are preparing for failure in life. Breaking old habits and promoting self-confidence are crucial activities that can get people on the road to success. Delay is very difficult to break and takes time to eradicate. However, if you understand the exact causes, it will be easier to figure out how to stop the delay.

Delay is a symptom, not the cause. And as with all symptoms, you need to identify and eliminate the root cause. Treating the symptom would mean taking painkillers constantly to worsen the pain over time due to the untreated root cause. The problem is that most people's advice on how to stop hesitating. People assume that just because something worked for their particular deferral case, it works for every possible case. However, the fact is that hesitation has many possible causes, and you need to find out what it causes to use the right remedy. The good news is that once you understand this principle, you can effectively fight the delay! Often you will hesitate when faced with a big task for one simple reason - you don't know what the next step is. You try to do the whole job at once, and this leads to an overwhelming feeling, which your mind escapes through hesitation. This is how you break down the task so that it is easy for your mind to digest. You'll want to break down a big, vague task into simple, actionable steps to overcome this kind of delay. (This works best if you have an example in mind.) First, let's answer a few questions: What is the bottom line you want to achieve? How do you know you've completed the task? What has to happen beforehand? And before? Keep going until you get a clear overview of everything that needs to happen before you can do your job. Then find out the next specific step you need to take. And make sure it's feasible.

Delay is a deadly disease. Delay kills not only your time but also your dreams and the chances you would have had for real success. If hesitation disturbs your lifestyle, you have to take a few steps to get your life under control. Simply put, you have to put an end to this delay. If you could stop the delay forever, wouldn't it be great? Think about how good your life would be if you had no more delay.

We guarantee that you will feel so much better and be even more successful. Those who hesitate tend to have feelings of fear, fainting, and guilt. Postponement is not something we have to live with. Whenever you have a delay in your life, you will never do anything. They will postpone things until tomorrow, and unfortunately, tomorrow will never come. If nothing is done, you will feel like you are useless in the world. Postponement can actually lead to severe depression. So really, how could you stop the delay in its place? First, you could organize yourself. By being organized and setting some schedules, you stop the delay. If you have a schedule, make sure you stick to it and don't let yourself down. Whatever you do, you should have some discipline. If you can't solve this problem on your own, you can always get someone to help you. If you stop hesitating, you will be much happier and on your way to success. You will see a completely different life before your eyes.

Have you ever had to sit down at the end of the day and say to yourself, "Where did the day go? I don't feel like I've accomplished anything today." If you are, you are like millions of other people on this wonderful planet of ours; you are a procrastinator! Delay is the reason why you are still in the place you were at this time last year. Delay is the reason why you are constantly living in the past or in the future. Procrastination is a dream theft! However, it is light at the end of the tunnel. Concentrate on one task at a time. Do not start thinking about your next task until you have completed the task at hand. Do not think about the previous task at all when you have continued with the next one. If the task you're working on is part of a larger project, set a specific goal for that period (e.g., read for half an hour or a certain number of pages, or brainstorm ideas). Whichever task you look at and immediately apologize for NOT doing, it is the task you should do first. Why? This way, you give yourself the momentum you need to complete your list with GUSTO! The feeling of success that you create when you first complete the most difficult task catapults your productivity to a stratospheric level.

Deleting your desktop means you can only concentrate on one task at a time. And approximate what? You've apparently heard it before; a tidy environment means a tidy mind. So get rid of those stacks of paper and keep your desk and thoughts FREE from clutter. Sometimes, if you feel like you're losing focus, you may just need to drink some water. Scientists have now proven beyond any doubt that regular fluid intake is essential for creativity. Therefore, make sure that you regularly take a 5 to 10-minute break from your work area and do sports like a short walk. A short 5-minute meditation also works very well. Create a reward system for yourself, and you will suddenly be much more inspired to put one foot after each other when it gets difficult. It sounds great, doesn't it? But most of us are probably not doing it consistently enough. It is a fantastic incentive to push a project forward. Do you think you will learn more if you are enthusiastic about the topic? Think back to your school days. Did you learn more from the educators who were enthusiastic about their subject or from those who only went through the applications? So even if you only count a few cents, even if you throw out the waste, do it with ardor, do it to the ideal of your ability, always bring positive energy to the task. Convince yourself through positive soliloquy that what you do is important for the great vision. The real key to this particular phase of the process of avoiding postponement is to be cognitively tempted to think what you are doing is just fantastically important to your success.

We can delay acting on something because we want it to be perfect. We reasonably know that nothing is perfect. However, it can sometimes be hard to discover a balance between perfect action and no action at all. Don't wait to start; start with what you have NOW, where you are now! Leave your comfort zone. That alone can be the biggest hurdle to overcome. Re-label "Procrastination" and use something else instead! Even the word "postponement" can have negative undertones. It is, therefore, vital that you change your attitude towards something more positive. For example, you have researched online on the Internet and searched for various websites. Now the thing is, you were originally only online to find some important details, but almost an hour later, you still haven't discovered the information you need. Now there are two options. You can get annoyed that you are wasting valuable time, OR you can call this time a break that was necessary to recharge your batteries and move forward. Then you take control of the negative emotions associated with postponing. You turned them over and used them to your advantage. So there you have it. Overcoming the delay is not easy, but it can be easy.

So what can we do about postponement, both for pedestrians and for ubiquitous people? Chronic delay is too big a problem for capacity hacks. Another option is to use negative impulse (punishment). This is the brute force method of overcoming deferral and works for a while. Inedible and bordering on self-abuse, but it can be effective. First, if you were already positively motivated, hesitation would not be a problem. So is there a way to "create" positive motivation, so to speak? Is it possible to be positively motivated even if you didn't start out like this originally? For example, once you've started a task, it's easier to maintain momentum. In fact, it feels good to continue working on a task or project, even if it's not a topic that you particularly like. Of course, starting a task or project itself can be a problem. Chronic deferral is clearly a harder nut to crack, as it is ubiquitous and consuming. Positive motivation also doesn't matter if the procrastinator is chronically resistant to attempts to approach the topic at all. Not everything is hopeless. Simple postponement and chronic postponement can be "treated," so to speak, by improving attention control and metacognition. If you can focus on the things that you are putting off - things that you may not be aware of - at least improve your chances. At best, you can master the challenges that you once found insurmountable. There are several ways to train attention. Meditation also helps you become more in tune with your emotions and become aware of the patterns and situations that can trigger them.

It seems that with all our willpower and our need for performance, we can take up the ideas for action that we have and implement them. You have the power to prevent others from performing flawlessly in time, but why are you stopping the performance? Why should you stop doing a task when it needs to be done? It seems a bit counterintuitive, at least. For those of us who hesitate, we'll be our worst best enemy. Think about it, you have a job to do, and all you have to do is do it. Nobody should stand in your way, but the day simply passes, and you haven't done the job. Each of us had these deferral times. And what do we get from it? Stress. Postponement is the act of postponing, Postpone or delay or postpone action until a later date. How many of us "put" tomorrow what we should do today? Whenever we hesitate, it destroys our productivity and kills our dreams. Just think about for a minute: what can you possibly achieve (what is it worth to be reached) if you don't take action? If you postpone cleaning your home, you will eventually live in a pigsty, not to mention the health problems that can result from poor maintenance. Postponement is a "deliberately and habitually postponing what should be done." Note that the postponement is intentional. So many people are betraying themselves into believing that postponement is something that simply "happens" without human effort or contribution. However, this is not true. You have to participate in hesitating actively. If you see that something needs to be done and you don't, take an active part in it and cause your own failure. Imagine that you feel like your body just isn't working properly, and you have plans to see a doctor. Your appointment is coming, and because you felt like you had worked hard all week and deserved some rest, you postponed it. A day turns into a week, a week into a month, and you just forget to leave at all. After passing out at work, you find that you have an illness that could have been prevented if you had only done what needed to be done. Don't let postponement kill you if you dream of being a success. There is no miracle solution for the postponement other than taking action. Taking the necessary measures, if necessary, is the only solution for the delay. Whenever you hesitate, you feel guilty and sometimes even depressed. It was found that people who lack the motivation to do even minimal tasks are borderline or manically depressed. You will always feel better after you get things done.

Postponement increases depression and can lead to poor health, bad relationships, poor grades, and poor work performance, which can attend to loss of employment. Nobody wants to see these things happen to them. So why are you hesitating? Detecting Deferment The first step in overcoming deferral is to acknowledge the existence of a deferral. You cannot get to "victory" until you realize that you have a problem for the first time. It's like having a medical problem. You cannot get the treatment you need until you have identified and diagnosed the problem "first." You can then continue to troubleshoot the problem.

Understand the "why" behind your postponement brings you closer to overcoming. Suppose you postpone cleaning your home. Maybe it's because you got it out of control so that it overwhelmed you, and you just wish it would go away. Postponement usually occurs when a task that needs to be done is not pleasant. Most people have no problem doing things that they enjoy — their human nature. We are designed to move away from pain and approach pleasure. Steps to Counteract Postponement is to Rethink and recognize that people are wired to move away from painful things, associate postponement with the consequences of not doing important things. Create a mental picture of the negative results that can occur if you don't do things. This mental shift can give you the motivation to "take action" to avoid the pain of the aftermath. Sometimes you can hesitate because it looks like there is so much to do - and yet so little time to get things done. One way to overcome this type of postponement is to prioritize. Make a note of a task list and then check which tasks are most important and which are least important. Then prioritize these tasks according to their importance. Responsible Partner, appointing someone to hold you accountable is another good way to counter the delay. We usually try to do what we say when we know someone else is watching us and holding us accountable. Set your priority list the night before. First of all, building your list in advance can help build confidence because you've got something done. You may also sleep better at night and look forward to the next day. Since we cannot predict tomorrow's events with any certainty, you should be ready to make some changes to your list if necessary.

Focus on the real problems - the underlying fears, attitudes, and irrational ideas. Next, identify the underlying problem. Start with the question: "Am I a relaxed or a tense procrastinator?" Tense procrastinators suffer from strong, sometimes evil internal critics. Relaxed procrastinators deny reality. The following are some self-help measures that should help relaxed and tense procrastinators. For most procrastinators, a to-be-done list, a daily schedule, and a simple logging and rewarding process are miracles. Changes can occur immediately, but relapse is common. Most people have to overcome the delay gradually. Break down large orders into manageable tasks and work on the first steps. Maybe do it yourself by saying, "I only do five minutes," and then find that you don't mind working longer than five minutes. This is known as a "five-minute plan." The key is to learn the habit of starting a task early. Divide large tasks or projects into smaller parts. Reward yourself for small successes - you deserve it. Don't punish yourself if you hesitate. You will eventually develop new habits with new feelings of self-confidence and performance. If you find this very difficult, contact an "anti-procrastination coach," who is usually a very good friend whom you have trusted and who will alert you if he finds you hesitant. Start with your day's important task FIRST and do all the other less important tasks of the day later. In short, most procrastinators are not lazy but can do all kinds of other tasks to postpone them - the most important task of the day. This is accomplished for a mixture of reasons, most of which are not excuses but excuses. These feelings of success are the feelings that help you drive changes in your behavior.A common problem that is usually explained as a delay in important tasks. Most of us hesitate at some point. What are other signs of a delay than waiting until the last minute to do something? Try these out: you don't want to take any chances or try something new, stay at home or in the same old job, get sick when faced with an unpleasant job, avoid confrontation or decisions, blame others or the situation ("it is boring"). For your misfortune or to avoid doing something, making big plans but never carrying them out, or having a busy schedule that makes it difficult to do important work. This list of symptoms suggests that the postponement, which initially sounds like simple behavior, is actually quite complex. It includes emotions, skills, thoughts, or attitudes, and factors that we do not know. In addition, the causes and dynamics of moving an important but uncomfortable task vary from person to person and from assignment to assignment for the same person. For example, you can postpone your math task but immediately fill out an application for school. If we understand how and why we hesitate, we can hopefully change that. Postponement is a strange anomaly. Its purpose seems to be to make our lives more enjoyable, but instead, it almost always adds stress, disorganization, and frequent failure. You want to get a result, usually, something that you and others appreciate and respect - "I have to start." You hesitate and think briefly about the real and imagined advantages of a later change. "I'll do it tomorrow if I don't have a lot to do. "You delay more, become self-critical - "I should have started earlier" - or apologize - you can hide or pretend to be busy; you can even lie about other obligations. You hesitate even more until the task has to be done, usually hastily - "Just let it get done in some way" - or you just don't have time - "I can't do this!" They insult themselves - "Something is wrong with me" - and swear never to hesitate again, or you ignore the importance of the task - "It doesn't matter." You repeat the process almost immediately for other important tasks as if it were an addiction or a compulsion.The smartest way to go about it would usually be to get the uncomfortable job done as quickly as possible while we have enough time to do the job properly and solve it without adding to our agony. But we put it off. Why? There are many possible reasons: We have a good feeling about setting goals and declaring that "at some point," we will change or be successful. By hesitating, we shorten the time that we actually need to complete the task. Most of the time, we avoid the unpleasant task at all. The best way to understand hesitation is to identify the emotions that are related to or underlying behavior. Procrastination is actually an attempt to deal with our emotional reactions. What are these sensations? Fear of failure or success is the most likely emotion Anger - this includes rebellion against control. Dislike of the work to be done is another. Depression can slow us down (and postponement failure can depress us). Looking for pleasure is another distracting motive. The task for the procrastinator is, therefore, to identify your form of procrastination correctly and to find a quick fix for your specific emotional reaction.

The procrastinator must learn to start learning and preparing for work and exams early on. However, many procrastinators oppose these methods. A really committed "relaxed" procrastinator needs more inner motivation, maybe a new philosophy of life, or just more care and tension, a much stronger self-critic. Relaxed procrastinators usually use three types of common distractions to avoid something. This does something that is not a priority, for example: watching TV, eating, playing, sleeping, or even cleaning. Once we are immersed in the distraction, we block the fear, self-doubt, anger, or boredom associated with the work that we postpone that we should do. Mental excuses. There are three major types: (a) "I'll do it tomorrow" or "I'll do my best work late at night, I'll do it then." Since you have promised yourself to be good, you can escape work and play without guilt. (b) "I'm going shopping now so I can study all evening" or "I'll call her as soon as I can think of something clever" or "I'll set up my apartment, and I'll make friends." Some unimportant activities take precedence over the main event, which is uncomfortable or scary. (c) "I want an 'A' in the statistics, but Dr. Mean would never give me one." 3. Emotional distractions. Drug use, listening to music, reading novels, and even participating in friendships, love relationships, flirting, or religions can sometimes serve as an escape from unpleasant but important tasks.

What can the pleasure-seeking procrastinator do? Stop turning small, uncomfortable molehills (like doing something uncomfortable) into huge mountains. Start thinking more rationally. You don't have to go to every celebration. You may be interested in project implementation. Make detailed, realistic plans to achieve your goal, and don't avoid the work, do it now! If you are a fear-based procrastinator, try to reduce your fear of failure. Keep records of avoiding important tasks: what excuses were used? What thoughts and feelings did you have? What was done instead of work? What was the result? Change hesitant mindsets to productive: 4. Take responsibility instead of blaming them. Productive people have to go on vacation and play (without feeling guilty)! Insist on your fun. Turn panics and self-doubts into assets by asking: what is the worst possible outcome? What would I do if the worst occurs? How would I go on? What courage and skills do I have that would help me deal with it? How will I excuse myself for messing up? What alternative plans could I develop for a good life? Can I do something now to avoid this terrible result that I fear? After I prepare for the worst, how can I prepare to become stronger and more productive? This type of planning helps us face the inevitable risks that await us all. Plan your fixed hours and your entertaining time. That is all, no work! Make gaming mandatory, not work. Work is more fun if it is not seen as hard, boring, and endless work that needs to be done. Other methods are required: a calendar based on when projects are due, a set of realistic goals, a relaxed focus, and a quick, optimistic response to setbacks. While most of the deferral issues can be resolved using the self-help methods listed above, the main issue is consistency and traceability.

WHAT IS DEFERMENT?

People hesitate to postpone activities that could, and in many cases, should be done now. Procrastinators delay activities until a later date. The term does not apply to those who have two equally important things to do and have to choose one first. Rather, it applies to people who have tasks or activities with clear priorities and who unnecessarily postpone the most important task or activity in order to delay it. Many psychologists believe that people often hesitate because of fear of starting or completing a project. Other psychological causes are low self-esteem and a self-destructive mentality. Mental illnesses, such as ADHD or depression, can also lead to delays. It is important to stop the delay. Internally, a person often feels stress, guilt, or fear when he hesitates. Externally, the person can be seen as lazy, unproductive, or disorganized. While it may be normal for a person to hesitate from time to time, it becomes a problem when it begins to affect a person's life. This type of behavior can cause a person to lose their job and seriously affect a person's life. It is extremely difficult to change a delayed pattern without help. However, it is often procrastinators who postpone seeking help to end the problem. Some procrastinators can delay the search for treatment because they do not want to investigate the reasons for the procrastination. NLP and Hypnotherapy, it is not constantly necessary or desirable to investigate why people hesitate. For this reason, the methods of neurolinguistics programming (NLP) and Hypnotherapy are successful treatment methods for some people. NLP and Hypnotherapy are not focused on why you hesitate but on how your thoughts keep you from doing what needs to be done. Together, NLP and Hypnotherapy focus on what needs to be achieved and motivate you to do these tasks. The target of NLP and Hypnotherapy is to get you to make changes in the way you think and respond, rather than focusing on the underlying cause. For many people, this is a convenient and effective way to stop delay problems and achieve personal and professional goals.

BODY LANGUAGE

People have a tendency to communicate with each other. This can be done in an obvious and not so obvious way. We speak, we write. But we can also communicate with each other without words. When words are used to communicate content, this non-verbal communication speaks about our relationships. This is probably more important than getting the message across. We communicate meta-communication skills via communication! When words just don't do it when we speak to a person, we also need to make it clear how to interpret the content of our message. The way we do this speaks about the relationship we have with that person, or at least the way we think about that person. Words cannot do that. It is easier to show than to talk about our emotions. The meaning of our words comes from body language. In de Saussurian meaning, this language (in contrast to the slogan) is used for non-verbal communication. We use it all the time. Most of the time, we are not conscious of it. Touching someone during a conversation means something completely different than not touching our conversation partner. It is simply not possible to communicate without non-verbal language - written words are the only exception. Are we aware of it? Most body language is communicated on an unconscious level. However, this has a major impact on the quality of our message. From this, we can conclude that it would be a good idea to become aware of others' body jargon - and more importantly. We can acquire the skill of how to use our body language for one purpose and to understand the body language of others. We also need to be aware that body language is interpreted culturally - its meanings differ in different cultures. The interpretation depends on the situation, the culture, the relationship to the person, and the gender of the other. This means that not a single signal from our body has the same meaning in all parts of the world. This is an important point and should be considered. The language of our body is holistically connected to the spoken language and our entire behavioral pattern. Various signals can complement each other to strengthen the importance of our communication. Some social groups have developed a certain body language, which is very clear because the use of words in a particular situation is difficult. These are mainly minorities in cultures where there is a great history of prejudice against the prevailing culture.

Body language - speak without words.

One of the most prominent types of communication that we use in our daily interactions is our non-verbal or body language. It is the type of communication that ignites our feelings and reactions at the intestinal level. Research has shown that learning an understanding of body language increases your ability to achieve anything you want in a given situation. Have you ever seen partners sitting together and having an idea of how good or bad their relationship was in minutes? Have you ever speculated how you could get this result so quickly without direct interaction? Even if you are aware of it or not, we spend our days responding to people's non-verbal signals projected through their body language and drawing results about them from our observations. Our body language reveals the truth we hide from the world in our words, including how we really feel, our relationships, and our situations. Through eye contact, gestures, posture, and facial expressions, the people we interact with determine our purposes, the quality of our relationships, how masterful we are in a particular situation, our self-confidence, and what our true motivations and desires are. The power of body language lies in the emotional response that it evokes. Feelings determine decisions and reactions in almost every situation. Non-verbal cues trigger feelings that determine an individual's core assets, such as truthfulness, trustworthiness, and sincerity, level of competence, and leadership qualities. The interpretation of these keywords can determine who we meet, what job we are hired for, what success we achieve, and who may be chosen in influential political positions. With such a decisive skill, why don't we spend years learning and developing effective body language skills? The truth is that most people underestimate the importance of body language until they seek a deeper understanding of human habits in a personal relationship or an advantage in a competitive business situation.

Mastering body language gives people the opportunity to interpret the meaning behind certain gestures and body movements and to understand how messages can be effectively projected and communicated in dealing with others. As a result, the overall effectiveness of interpersonal relationships is greatly increased. The best way to start this process of mastery is to learn the basic interpretation of the two core types of body language - open presence and closed presence. The body language of the closed presence is used in people who fold their bodies around the midline of the body, which runs from the top of the head to the feet in the middle of the body. The physical characteristics that create this type of presence are feet that are close together, arms close to the body, hands crossed or held together in front of the body, small hand movements close to the body, shoulders rolled forward, and eyes down par. The messages the body language of the closed presence sends to the world are lack of self-confidence, low self-esteem, fainting, and lack of experience. In extreme cases, you can even generate the message that you want to be invisible. The effects on the individual who projects this type of body language can range from simply not the best possible opportunities to a worst-case scenario in which there is a self-fulfilling view of victimization. In contrast, the open presence is evident in people who develop a sense of authority, power, and leadership by projecting self-confidence, success, strength, and skill. The physical characteristics are feet that are hip-wide apart, open hand movements that are used in conversations outside the body's midline, elbows that are kept away from the body, restrained shoulders, straight positions, and eyes that are aimed at the listener's eye level, These people are seen as attractive, successful, intelligent, and seem easy to succeed. We consider this body language type as the "body language of the leaders." Eye contact is key to improve body language and project an open presence. Eye contact is one of the vital means of communication we have. Direct eye contact when interacting with others can change the way people see them. When people start speaking directly into someone's eyes, they are seen as confident, trustworthy, and competent.

Hand gestures and facial expressions are the second levels of change that can be made to be seen with an open presence. These types of communication lend themselves to improving the ability to communicate messages clearly and effectively. The skillful use of open hand movements outside the body and expressive facial features achieve a greater effect when speaking by visually stimulating the listener and increasing the amount of information provided during the interaction. Even as a child, we are taught that good boys and girls sit well with their legs folded and their hands folded in front of them. The encouragement to control physical space as children can produce some of the characteristics of the body language of the closed appearance in adulthood. In order to counteract this effect, one can begin to take over the characteristics of the body language of the open presence and to integrate these manners into their natural state of being. Once this behavior change is complete, the same non-verbal impressions and messages are displayed as with the open presence. Mastering body language is critical to creating the most effective presence in all interpersonal interactions. People without this command tend to be misunderstood and find their efforts to communicate their ideas unsuccessful. With the ability to distinguish between the different modes of body language, anyone can gain the necessary mastery to succeed in any company they choose.

However, it would be wrong to assume that most of the communication is through body language. In everyday life, we usually don't negate what people say. So what becomes interesting about body language and how body language becomes useful depends on what is said. In patients with advanced dementia, physical appearance is an important factor in assessing pain due to the limited ability to communicate verbally. In almost all other cases, a nurse would not rely on how a patient behaved to indicate how much pain a patient was in; they would ask the patient. If someone is sitting with their arms and legs crossed and has an annoyed expression on their face, you probably won't speak to them. In this case, body language is 100% communication, but the only way to ensure this is to speak to them. Body language betrays you by revealing your feelings and attitudes, but it is your words and their relationship to your body language that are really central to your communication. Despite the importance of body language in communication, non-verbal communication without the verbal part of communication is very limited. It's the combination of words and body language that betrays you, especially when what you say and how you act doesn't match. If someone says that they are happy but not acting happily, you don't need a book on body language to be able to read the characters better. Even if the person you spoke to did not read the books, it is very likely that your body language will betray you.

When you dare to deal with other people on a daily basis, you don't have to worry about how you behave, but how you behave in relation to what you say. Your body language can be unpredictable and excited when you say exciting things, but when you act erratically when you lie, the situation is different. But if you are telling the truth, why do you want to fake body language? The answer is simple that we are only human. When we say nice things to our partners or talk to our superiors, we are sometimes just too tired or just not interested. We can talk about the one thing we think is the most interesting or exciting in the world, but if we are hungry or tired or sick or just have a bad day, the words we use may be enthusiastic, but our body language will betray us. How do you fake it? Most experts say you can't fake body language. But trying to look good could be a problem. So what do we do? The simple answer is that we increase the mismatch between what we say and our body language. We increase mismatch in two ways: The first thing we can do is be honest. Don't try to sound too enthusiastic if you aren't. If you feel tired, do not try to compensate for this through excessive arousal. You can be excited, but don't do it too much. If you disagree with someone, don't lie to them. Avoid answering them directly as much as possible. So if your girlfriend or boyfriend asks, "Do I look fat in it?" answer with "you look good" or "you look good in this dress" and then try to change the subject.

Whether you say yes or no, you are probably lying. So don't answer the question. Don't avoid the topic, but don't answer the question directly. The second thing we can do is be aware of how you are behaving and do something else. Congruence is about continuity. If you have any doubts about the continuity of the signs, you should be able to make it difficult to read and thus disrupt congruence. Although telling the truth can be a delicate matter, you need to think about how you feel and know something about body language to disrupt the congruence of your body language. Not much information is required, but you should be aware that body language usually works in clusters. So what you do with your arms is only relevant if it relates to the expression on your face and your way. If you need to make sure that someone in your body language doesn't read everything about you, you want to break up the clusters of your actions and, as a result, disrupt congruence.

Areas of body language that you should focus on: Facial expressions: if you're bored, show interest, if you're happy, show a little sadness, if you have nothing to say, do it as if you wanted to say something, If someone you speak to gives you the opportunity to speak and you don't, they will start to question their own understanding of you. Eye contact: Failure to maintain eye contact indicates a lack of interest or deception. Aggressively maintained eye contact shows the desire to dominate another person. Assess your own feelings and intentions and adjust eye contact accordingly. Touch: The attraction is indicated by physical touch. When a woman in a dating situation starts touching another person, she shows interest in them. Avoid inappropriate touching. In the workplace, inappropriate touch is more than a handshake. Touch in interpersonal relationships. You may feel tempted, but your partner will really appreciate this hug. Arms and legs: Your posture reveals all sorts of things about you. Two elements to consider are showing arms and legs and open or closed posture. We often show interest in someone by putting our arms and legs on them. If we are not interested and ready to go, we can point our limbs at the door to be ready when the time comes to go. On a very simple level, the open or closed posture is the difference between crossed arms and legs and uncrossed arms and legs. The closed body says, "I'm not interested, or I'm listening." An open body says the opposite. Tone: How do you speak normally? Are you a loud, fast speaker, a slow, quiet speaker? Think about your behavior when you're angry. Don't get carried away too much. You don't want the boss to think you're aggressive when you're just tired; you want to think about volume, speed, tone, and fill your voice with a bit of emotion. Your body language will betray you. An uncontrollable mismatch between what you do and what you say is that you say something you don't want. Think about what you are about to say and how you feel, and then do something completely different. A small disturbance goes far.

Man is a "social animal" and a "language animal." It is hard to believe when psychologists claim that 90% of our communication is not verbal at all. The meaning of this fact is simple: we communicate and convey many messages without saying a word. Life and death are in the hand of the tongue, but once we realize that 90% of our communication is non-verbal, we must also be aware of the messages we convey in our non-verbal communication, such as they affect those around us. Disrupting body language can be hard work and is not something you want to do all the time. If you regularly use it on an unusually attentive friend, they will pick up your signals and see through your strategy. If you disturb congruence, if you feel insecure, you can defend yourself against the betrayal of body language. How do athletes get better? Players learn to pass, kick, shoot, attack, stop, change direction, close running lines, and many other skills. If you improve these skills, they will be better and more effective in the game. You improve these skills for two reasons: Non-verbal communication in sport If the psychologists are not wrong and 90% of our communication is actually non-verbal, why not use the method of sport improvement in relation to non-verbal communication? After all, this is a crucial skill for the strength of the team, which also affects the playing field during the game, during breaks, in the changing room, and during training. The use of non-verbal communication in the group takes place at every team player meeting and during the entire meeting. The responsibility of the players and coaches is also, and perhaps primarily, to be aware of themselves and to learn to communicate positively. Negative body language and team composition that a team has to let go of a player, no matter how good he is, if he constantly "poisons" the group atmosphere with a negative body language.

Universal Body Language Studies indicate that body language is a universal language that crosses cultures, genders, or physical limitations. How do you change negative body language? Show them the clip in private and discuss their feelings with them. Sometimes such a reflection would do the trick. Make it clear that you may feel "fake" first. That the gap between what they feel and what they express is legitimate. However, what they express is more important because it affects the team. If the player has not been able to get rid of their negative body language, ask them for professional help and take a clear position on the subject. Part of everyone's perception is their ability to read body language. Although we make extensive use of our sense of sight, smell, and touch, we also rely on subtle cues that are mostly registered unconsciously. How would you like to be ready to consciously read another person's nonverbal cues and develop your own? Would you like to be a specialist in body language flirting? How many times have you met someone whom you have "warmed up" naturally? Have you ever been in the presence of someone who made you shiver, or did you immediately like it for no apparent reason? Have you ever suspected someone of lying for delivering your speech in a way that was not convincing? Have you ever seen someone you were instantly attracted to by moving or talking, rather than by their looks or what they said? This is body language that flirts at work. Everyone reads other people's non-verbal cues. We unconsciously look at others by matching their language and what they do with their body language. Males sometimes find it difficult to read non-verbal cues in others. Men are very much dominated by their heads and have less contact with their emotional sides. When women are dominated by emotions, they are more aware of the emotional signs that are normally represented by their body language. We all, even if we are not aware of it, give signals that indicate how we think and what our intentions are. The body language of a man or woman can tell you numerous things about them if you know how to read them. Everyone flirts with body language to some extent, even if they don't know they are doing it. Women are notoriously good at judging a man's intentions. You usually do this by looking at his body language and comparing it to what he says. Men find that much more difficult.

Flirting in body language and your current mindset determines any form of non-verbal communication. Your mindset is determined by how you think and what you feel. It is possible to learn how to use your body to represent everything you want - especially when flirting in body language. Some courses can teach you the correct posture, hand gestures, tonality of the voice, etc. These courses use a forced approach to flirting in body language and can be difficult to master. However, there is a simple and faster way. There is a way that you can read and present the best body language flirting techniques without having to do a lot of work. While flirting in body language depends on how you think and feel, you just have to control these two things. This way, your body language can flirt naturally and is therefore much more powerful and attractive. It's much easier than you might think! You can do this by generating certain emotions in yourself, by thinking of certain thoughts. This can be both extremely entertaining and productive. Flirting in body language can be controlled through a simple process of mental images, better known as visualization. Imagine being confident and comfortable around attractive people. This way, you can trigger positive natural reactions in your body. Now imagine that you are confident, charming, and attractive to potential partners. See yourself in your mind's eye as a charismatic approach to people. Can you imagine how that would feel? After a few minutes of this mental exercise, imagine that you are actually entering the "other" you. Feel how good it feels that you are new and enjoy these feelings. This trains your body to be confident, and flirting in body language becomes natural.

An inferiority position by verbally, physically, and emotionally agreeing too much with an individual or group. Another inferiority position by trying to get an individual or group to agree with you.

Neither approval nor search for approval. Rather, it is a series of indications of superiority - position of power in non-verbal and verbal communication. It can also be a position of neutrality. Imagine that you are equipped with a camera around the clock. As we have noticed, women notice everything when it comes to men in a social environment. So if you turn around to stare at a hot girl who just passed by, you've just discredited yourself with all the other girls in the room. Only simple postures can go a long way. Did your mother always tell you to lean your shoulders back and walk with confidence? Well, she was right about that. Always keep that in mind and get in touch with yourself to see how to deal with it. Have a good smile, but don't overdo it. However, this makes you too close, and you may overcompensate for nervousness or fear. Smiling creates a positive aura, makes it easier to get closer, and prevents you from becoming creepy unless you smile too much, of course. Always have good, positive conversations with people around you, including strangers, but not out of nervousness. So your body language remains relaxed. You never want to look tight. This has advantages on several levels. If there is an opportunity to talk to you while you are in the prospect's view, just consider all of the body language improvements mentioned above.

Feelings are important

Body language is particularly used to express feelings. For example, when we like someone, it is often difficult to tell the person directly. On the other hand, it is easier to clarify our feelings (intentionally or unintentionally) through body language. The opposite is also true. We can say that we are angry with words, but our body language can say loud and clear that we are NOT. This can be very complex for the recipient of the message. The situation is usually described as issuing double messages - one message in words and one opposite message in body language. It is also difficult to cover up or lie about our feelings through body language. We can reveal their true feelings by not being aware of their body language. Research has shown that the majority of people pay more attention to their impressions of how a person acts through body language and believe in it rather than what is said by words. As a result, we tend to question the spoken words if they do not correspond to body language awareness of how we communicate. Only a small part of the way we meet another person is determined by the words we speak. It is vital that we know and master our body language (to a certain extent). The recipient of our body language will have a feeling that is often difficult to describe, put into words, or prove that something has been communicated. But it was. We all said to each other with certainty: "I don't think he/she likes me" or "I don't really believe what was said." It's called intuition, and body language plays a very big role because it gives us ideas about the other person that we can clarify on an intuitive level. We have to get to know our own body language first. We should learn it so that we can recognize it in others as well as in ourselves.

Know and understand your body language

Whether you notice it or not, body language is an important factor in how everyone you meet gets an opinion about you. In many professions, especially those where you help others, listening skills are a must and very important to build good relationships with customers. Whether you're helping people maintain their personal relationships, guiding people to succeed in business, or advising them on other issues, they see your body language and show that good listening skills make people more comfortable. Bad body language can cause you to miss something big. It is not so important that you hear every word carefully and honestly. It is your body language that makes them feel important and that you give them the attention they need. Here it is valued to know what the signs of a bad listener are, and you should try to get rid of them. If you have a manner of crossing your arms over your chest, or if you are impatiently tapping your toes, leaning, or turning away too often, or looking here and there all the time while listening, then tell the other person that you are not interested in what he or she says. This will most likely lead to the end of the business relationship and can lead to enormous business losses. So how can you make your body language send positive signals to the person you're talking to? First, you should try to turn to the other square of people. Don't look away to send a positive signal. Then we come to the posture of your body at the time of communication. You should be open-minded. You should never keep your arms or legs folded. Otherwise, the other person believes that you are not interested in listening to their point of view.

If you lean forward while talking to someone, your body language says you pay more attention to what he or she is saying. If you lean against it, you have no interest at all. Then we come into eye contact. Eye contact is the most important factor. Always try to keep eye contact normal. If you look further down or look away, it shows that you are not interested in the matter and feel uncomfortable. In addition, the importance of a relaxed posture should not be overlooked. Try not to be too stiff. You should also not be too formal when speaking to someone. If you feel that you have suffered great losses from poor body language in the past, you should immediately start practicing the tips above. Your body language speaks for you as soon as you leave your home. Even if you don't speak, how you stand, how you sit, and how you use your hands, others perceive this as communication. So if you don't have a clear understanding of body language, sometimes your body language doesn't match your intentions, and people will get the wrong message. If your body language contradicts your intentions, it can mean a great loss to you as you lose credibility. So What Should You Do to Maintain Your Credibility? We should first learn a little more about body language to be more believable and competent in the eyes of others. Whenever you meet your customers for any type of business, make your listing as positive as possible. How can you do that? Talk about the business first as soon as you enter the customer's premises. Search the papers or your briefcase to make a negative impression. Even if you have to wait, it's best to read a magazine.

Another important tip on body language is that you should shake hands warmly and firmly. Next, we come to the choice of the chair we want to sit on. You should never state that you will only sit when the other person asks you to. Instead, you should choose the most suitable chair and sit down immediately. However, never make the mistake of sitting too close or too far away from the customer. How much space you should keep depends on the personality of the customer. A shy person wants to sit further away than an outgoing person. However, the perfect distance is between 20 and 50 inches. You can lean forward to get closer to the customer if you try to highlight a particular point. Eye contact is another essential part of body language. Eye contact and a smile on your face convey the message that you are an honest, sincere, and open person. Vague eye contact and a look around repeatedly send the message that you don't have enough confidence. However, also avoid constantly staring at the other person as this makes the customer feel quite uncomfortable. Always try to speak in your usual voice. When your voice is full of passion, it immediately catches the customer's attention.

Your tone is much more indispensable than the actual words you use. Body language refers to how you say your words, not what you actually say. If you speak in your normal tone, and the volume is also in the normal range, your body language can be considered excellent. A well-modulated voice with a normal rhythm and frequency is a sign of professionalism, interest, and passion. The sentences you use when speaking should be as straightforward as possible. On the other hand, if you use "um" or "ah" or clear your throat unnecessarily, it sends a signal that you feel anxious. If you want to develop your body language, you should also focus on your gestures and postures. You should always be open, take light and determined steps with your arms swinging, but stand upright. If you keep eye contact with the other person, hold your chin between your thumb and fingers, or touch the bridge of your nose with your hands or hit your chin, you show that you really care about what is said. On the contrary, bad body language implies nervous movements that indicate a lack of attention. You must avoid looking anxious and finding out about the message you are communicating with body language.

Non-verbal body language makes up about 90% of our communication as a person. We communicate a lot of information about our inner emotional states that can strengthen our verbal communication or even contradict our verbal communication, and a lot has been written about how to read body language and how to use it to determine whether a person is telling the truth or not in a survey for example or in a relationship. For example, revealing the secret can be very helpful in dealing with the feeling of disgrace since disgrace can be appropriate or inappropriate and inadequate. The way that tells you that you are a "bad" person can really limit your life. Non-verbal body language is, therefore, a signal and can reveal tendencies rather than truths. Can you manipulate non-verbal body language? Only if we allow ourselves to be manipulated as viewers. We need to keep a close eye on the people we are close to and maybe ask questions if the words we hear do not match the non-verbal body language. The mismatch may simply be an attempt to avoid a conflict on the matter, but we draw our conclusions and act faster than we can remember that we are committed to love, honor, and obedience, which means trusting us to recall.

We grow up with an excellent understanding of body language. The development of this understanding begins in the infancy of our communication with nurses. If you have ever had a lively animated baby in your hand and looked at it and listened to it, they are working very hard to get in touch with the caregivers. These babies know that it is vital to keep the people who feed them in touch. So they look adorable and act so that the oxytocin flows. Stress hormones flow quickly when the baby indicates that it needs to be changed or is hungry, and a scream of fear will motivate a parent's movement in no time. Non-verbal communication reinforces verbal communication, and we all learn to describe what we consultants refer to as congruence or incongruity in the coordination between verbal and physical communication as we gain life experience. We often say that the person who is incongruent lies about every question we have asked them. The only thing to think about when understanding body language is that your body language is constantly changing, especially in intimate relationships. For example, record someone who talks to you and your partner on Sunday morning and look at the very subtle messages that are later shown by the facial expression and tone of voice. You will see how the give and take are involved in a conversation about the usually banal events. When people feel stronger, body language and tone can, of course, be enhanced. There is a figure of experts who offer us their guide to body language, but even the experts can only observe and catalog one anomaly, and then they have to ask a question about the anomaly.

The next question is, of course, have you decided to demonstrate behavior based on the feeling that follows your perception of your communication? Perhaps we will next examine the consequences of this choice. Men move when asked to answer a specific question – the facial expression changes, which is obvious, and sometimes a moment or two. Most men do not feel at risk if they interpret the object as someone else. Other men have described collecting energy to escape, even though they remain calm. Understanding body language is a very fluid experience and the best feeling for dealing with others where feelings and behaviors can change incredibly quickly. If you need an instrument that can better grab your attention, go for training. It has a lasting impact on your attention, your memory, and even your IQ. It takes a good memory to pay attention to the ups and downs of communication and makes you an expert in understanding body language. Every time you chat with someone, watch the gestures they make. There will often be patterns and repeated ways of using gestures. Notice how certain gestures accompany certain words and sentences. Also, consider what they are doing with this gesture. When you listen to someone, you add or emphasize their hands to what they are telling you or what they are trying to communicate. You can watch them paint pictures in the air and interact with their imaginary world as they speak. These gestures are deep communications that come directly from our subconscious. So if you decide to recognize gestures, you're communicating with someone's subconscious and processes that wonderful stuff.

Once you notice a person's gestures, return some of them to the person. If you're referring to something they said, use your gesture too. This is known as mirroring or matching. Do not make it too accessible and not to imitate the person. It has often been described as drawing attention and communicating with someone's subconscious to build a relationship with someone. When you reflect their gestures back to them, a person's subconscious knows that you've noticed. If somebody moves his hand in circles while describing how it rotates, you can move your finger in circles to subtly mirror it. So this person, you don't know who she is, and you're looking forward to meeting." When you refer to them, you agree with their gesture and point in the same direction. Just like mirroring, this sends a covert message to the person that you understand what is going on with them and that you often understand better than that person's awareness! Examine how you can relate to people's gestures by doing this more and more. If someone says, "I want to do one thing, but something else is stopping me" while holding one of his hands in front of you, you could mark the hand and ask him, "What is it?" Sometimes people will just look at you curiously and say, "What do you mean?" But sometimes there is astonishment - the person becomes aware of things that they did not previously know about. It can really have a magical effect. Full engagement with people's gestures is not suitable for all situations, and there are many situations in the workplace where any type of physical contact is considered inappropriate. However, if you find yourself in a situation where you think it is appropriate and have a good relationship with the person who is okay with it, try it.

In the business and professional environment, people also use a lot of gestures, so you can subtly mirror those gestures to establish a relationship. In addition, users use gestures to describe a specific problem. Pay attention to the signs of others, their body language in communication, and reuse them for those who use them. Become aware of the purpose they serve and show that you understand and empathize with them.

FRUSTRATION

When your index finger points at something, you show your frustration with your body language. Wringing out your hands, playing with your hair, and clenching your hands tightly are also signs of your frustration. How does someone show that they feel bored? If the listener's eyes are not on the person speaking, when he is in a sloppy posture, or when he is doing something other than listening to what is being said, he is bored. The importance of body language continues to grow when you meet people from different cultures. A better solution is to be aware of mind control techniques. If you know how to work on your mind and are clear about how you get distracted, you are in control.

Suppression refers to the inability to access information based on its emotional meaning rather than the true loss of information. It has been found that a misinformation effect (false memories) occurs when actual memories are combined with the content of suggestions from other information sources, e.g., for example, when you are talking to other people who have experienced the same event, or when you are accessing new information from the media. Selective attention focuses on an event while filtering out irrelevant events. With continued attention, cognitive activity is focused on an event over a longer period of time. Shared attention refers to the simultaneous focus on two or more events. The feature integration theory claims that through targeted visual attention, an object can be perceived as a whole and not as a meaningless cluster of features. A pervasive pattern of distrust and mistrust, in which the person consistently interprets the motives of others as malicious, is characteristic of paranoid personality disorder. The main difference between paranoid personality disorders and psychotic disorders in which paranoia is involved is that paranoid personality disorders do not have delusions, whereas psychotic disorders do. People with schizoid personality disorder are pervasively indifferent to social relationships, express a limited range of emotions in social situations, often prefer to be "loners," and usually function appropriately in non-social situations. The schizotypal personality disorder is characterized by a pattern of social and interpersonal deficits that includes serious inconvenience and a limited ability to relate, perceptual and cognitive bias, and strange/eccentric behavior. People with Histrionic Personality Disorder are often sexually seductive, have exaggerated, if flat, feelings that change quickly, are easily influenced by others, seek constant confirmation/praise, and consider relationships to be closer than they really are.

People with a narcissistic personality disorder, often plagued by fantasies of power and success, show a pattern of magnificence, admiration, and lack of empathy that can lead to exploitative relationships. A borderline personality disorder is characterized by a pattern of instability in interpersonal relationships, self-image and affects significant impulsiveness (e.g., suicide threats, substance use) and fear of abandonment/control. The dominant defense mechanisms of a person with borderline personality disorder are division, idealization, and projective identification. A person with antisocial personality disorder must have had behavioral disorder symptoms 15 years ago and show a pattern of negligence and violation of other rights. Some symptoms are lack of remorse/empathy, impulsiveness, irritability, and aggressiveness as well as deception. Another term used to refer to people diagnosed with an antisocial personality disorder is a sociopath. An avoidable personality disorder is characterized by a persistent pattern of social inhibition, feelings of inadequacy, and hypersensitivity to negative evaluation, which leads to limited social contacts despite longing for contact and relationships. A dependent personality disorder is diagnosed when there is a pervasive and excessive need that leads to attachment, submissive behavior, and separation anxiety. People with this disorder often struggle to make decisions and take responsibility for their lives. Typically, code dependency refers to the intentional or accidental support of one person for another person's addiction or dependency. The obsessive-compulsive personality disorder is characterized by a constant preoccupation with perfectionism, order, and intellectual and interpersonal control, which severely limits openness, flexibility, and efficiency. Preventing unacceptable impulses by expressing the opposite is a defense mechanism that people diagnosed with obsessive-compulsive disorder are most likely to rely on. The dissociative fugue is characterized by unexpected travel from home or work, the inability to remember some or all of his past, and confusion about personal identity or the adoption of a new identity. Dissociative identity disorder (formerly multiple personality disorder) occurs when a person develops at least two identifiable personality states that repeatedly take control of the person's behavior, and the person is unable to access important personal information.

THE POWER OF POSITIVE REINFORCEMENT

Much has been written about positive reinforcement as psychology for performance changes. It is a technique that is used both in the education of animals and in the development of children and has now proven to be effective in the context of personnel management in company tools. How can you apply and monitor positive reinforcement as a business manager? First, understand that everyone likes to be recognized if they do a good job. Just pointing out if someone does something wrong and doesn't recognize what is done right can lead to negative results. Employees who are praised for doing things right or making progress in improving performance will work harder to do their jobs better. Employees who are not told when to do a good job and who are corrected or ridiculed when they do a bad job will only do the work that is required to stop causing trouble in the future. These employees can enjoy their work, improve their attitudes, or see a reason to work harder because poor performance is recognized. With this understanding of human behavior, managers must begin to change the approach to recognizing employees. Managers need to determine when an employee is doing something right and simply and sincerely praise him for what he has done. Tell the employee what he did right and how it helps the department or company. Let employees know that management has confidence in their ability to continue to perform well and to innovate in their own roles. This positive reinforcement of the employee's efforts should occur as soon as possible after it has been determined that the job is well done. Frequent, sincere, and positive praise can make a great contribution to ensuring that employees do their best.

Positive reinforcement does not mean that what an employee does wrong is ignored. Instead, this means first recognizing which part of the work was done correctly and then checking what can be done better next time and why the performance or work result did not quite meet expectations. If this means that the manager has to take part of the blame for not giving detailed instructions for the desired behavior or outcome, he should apologize and then explain how the manager will personally try to do better. This is a great time for the manager to tell the employee that he still has confidence in him but needs his help and cooperation by asking questions if the manager's instructions are not clear. In this way, employees and supervisors can communicate better, which leads to better completion of the tasks. Remember that managers must first deliver positive results, then track what improvements are needed, apologize when necessary, and then reaffirm what has been done correctly. Do not use the word "but" when working with the improvement or aftercare statement, as this word often negates everything that has been said before, and the employee may stop listening because he knows that a negative will come next. Understanding that everyone likes to be recognized when they do a good job is a typical human response that should help improve performance. Business managers need to learn how and when to apply positive reinforcement when monitoring improvements in work behavior or job performance. Managers should always take positive aspects into account instead of just mentioning when employees work below the desired level. Positive reinforcement could be the key to better results in HR management, which should also lead to better business results. It is also important to set positive impulses in our everyday life beyond workouts. The Secret is no longer a big secret, and parts of it agree: staying positive in life is a great way to get through your day. If you encounter negativity that brings you down, take a few deep breaths and re-frame them. Find the positive. It is always there. And with that, we can overcome pretty much any obstacle that blocks our way.

NLP

What is NLP?

NLP is the practice of neuro linguistic programming, a study of psychotherapy that includes interpersonal communication. NLP monitors facial expressions, body language, posture, and language to determine what a person is really saying. This form of study is useful in a number of areas, including business and sales, therapy, and treatment and management of diseases. Communication is not just a spoken word; it is also expressed through movement, posture, eyes, etc. The underlying principle of NLP is based on understanding what a person communicates. For example, a person who has emotional difficulties can express themselves more in their body positioning than in language. It is argued that studying neuro linguistic programming itself is more complicated than 30-minute television commercials. The practice is not a quantifiable, static study, but a dynamic and evolving one. The study of neurolinguistic programming is not widely recognized by the medical mainstream. A person with NLP authorization may have met different standards. NLP is the study of how people establish their thinking, feeling, language, and behavior in order to achieve the results they achieve. Modeling is the focus of much of the NLP, but there are also the patterns and techniques that come from the modeling projects. NLP patterns are a synthesis of powerful change measures, language models, and behavioral designs that are based on self-improvement and the achievement of excellence. The NLP patterns were modeled by geniuses who achieved amazing results in the fields of psychiatry, psychology, and psychotherapy. Patterning developed into a modern NLP with new modeling projects that stimulated new patterns and techniques over the years.

Neuro refers to our nervous system and how it processes information and encodes it as a memory in our body/neurology. With Neuro, we describe the experience as input, processed, and ordered by our neurological mechanisms and processes.

Linguistically means that the neural processes of the mind are coded, ordered, and given meaning by language, communication systems, and various significant systems (grammar, mathematics, music, icons). Programming assigns to our ability to organize our sensory information (sights, sounds, sensations, smells, tastes, and symbols or words) in our mind-body organism in order to achieve the desired results. Taking control of your own mind is at the heart of NLP. NLP is famous for the skills it offers to bring about adequate and lasting change. For instance, NLP has a technique called The Fast Phobia Cure. With this technique, NLP can cure a phobia in a very short time (often in 10-15 minutes). We used the procedure to cure phobias of water, bees, elevators, heights, public lectures, small places, airplanes, etc. Rapid phobia healing is just one of many techniques for such a change. We used a technique called timeline processes to remove traumatic images from the minds of traumatized people. In addition, we often use certain NLP techniques in conversation, which means that we do not have to use these techniques openly "therapeutically." Neuro-Linguistic Programming (NLP) examines the inner functions of the human mind; How we think, how we develop our wishes, goals, and fears and how we motivate ourselves, make connections and give our experiences meaning.

NLP presents specific skills and patterns required to make positive changes, make new decisions, deal with others more effectively, break away from old habits, self-destructive patterns, and behaviors, and think more clearly about what we want and how we can achieve it. - The relationship between mind, language, emotions, and behavioral patterns. It is a psychology of interpersonal and intrapersonal intelligence and communication. It includes findings from behavioral and Gestalt psychology, family therapy, hypnotherapy, linguistics, information theory, and anthropology. NLP started by examining people who are exceptionally good at what they do and figuring out how to do them so everyone can do the same can achieve similar results. It aims to go beyond correcting changes (correcting specific problems) to a "generative" change that enables you to do more in every area of your life. People often find that problems disappear or appear less important when they learn a new skill or make a breakthrough in one area of their lives. NLP stands for neurolinguistic programming. NLP is a school of various psychological techniques that communicate directly with the unconscious. The unconscious is very powerful, much more than our consciousness. What can NLP do? The best way to describe what NLP does is to upgrade the mind. You can improve your way of thinking, your intelligence, your memory, your senses, your appearance, and your communication skills. You can acquire the ability to improve, improve, or modify EVERY aspect of yourself or another. NLP can be a very powerful tool when used correctly. You can use NLP on yourself as well as on other people, and there are hundreds of ways to do it every day. You can even apply NLP to other people without them realizing it! However, it is easier to apply neuro linguistic programming to yourself.

Let's say you have to remember to take bread and milk with you on your way home. You could try saying to yourself, "Don't forget to pick up bread and milk!" Again and again, but this sentence contains the command "forgot to pick up bread and milk." Instead, it is much more likely that you will be successful if you tell yourself that you should remember to take bread with you. There are hundreds of tiny tricks that we can use in neuro linguistic programming. Standard definitions of NLP and even the outdated name Neuro-Linguistic Programming really do not do justice to what the modern concept has developed from. The unfortunate have deviated from their training and believe that NLP is just a set of techniques they have learned to serve a self-serving purpose. How much value have they missed, and their view is obscured by the fog of processes and procedures! NLP is so much more than just a set of techniques. NLP is a compelling way to be, a whole new way of being me and living the life that belongs to me. A new way of thinking that goes far beyond the limits of your existing neurology and leads to a quantum world of endless possibilities. Suddenly the light bulb flickered, and everything and everything became possible. NLP thinking begins with an opening of the mind and with a conscious and unconscious integration, bypassing the critical barrier of skills that blocks creativity and imagination and locks us firmly in logic. Who are we to impose our model of the world, our limited reality on others? If we let go of the chains that restrict our thinking, we will be able to take a look at the world without judgment, with honesty, trust, and forgiveness, and with a new respect for life.

Abruptly and perhaps suddenly, relationships take on a whole new quality. There are three main categories of relationships; Relationships to yourself, to others, and to our environment. The first impression of change arises in the primary relationship, the relationship to the self. Eventually, internal conflicts are resolved without either side being punished or defeated, but with a mutual consensus of the highest positive intent. Congruence is achieved through complete alignment, and the flows of energy start flowing again in fast currents. The dams that stopped the flow of energy for so long are destroyed and replaced by a cleansing immersion in self-confidence and contentment. Accepting others increases our relationships with new levels. By looking at each relationship from different perception platforms, it becomes easy to see views that are different from ours. Out of the blue, relationships become so much more interesting. When we change the way we speak to people, both verbally and non-verbally, connections are created, which means that everyone can really hear what we say and what we hear. If you treat every communication in a new way and with astonishment, relationships emerge that last for everyone in every context and in every environment.

Our relationship with our environment, whose vast universe we only occupy as a spot. As our NLP thinking evolves, it becomes clear that a crystal reflects the world on its glittering, multifaceted surface in the same way, and each precious individual projects its own reality. When we accept that we create our reality based on our own beliefs, values, and perceptions, we get the unique ability to shape and shape our reality. Projecting success is where success is understood. Knowing what we want, knowing what action we need to take to achieve it, and knowing when to act appropriately can welcome success and excellence in everything we do. Quantum physics tells us that every point in the universe is undeniably connected. Whatever you think you are, you are much, much more. NLP is about a thirst for knowledge. Supported by continuous learning steps that satisfy the desire for knowledge and self-image, we consistently push against the limits that define our thinking. We begin to expand our neurology and open up areas of the mind that have been lost to us for so long. Enlargement enables us to see new things in new ways and to go beyond what we think is possible. As the comfort zones expand, we develop the ability to understand what makes people tick, and the behavior they produce and change becomes possible. Increasing our mental capacity for ethical and desirable change within psychology leads to control over the state, physiology, and behavior that produced miraculous results. NLP has been regarded as the domain of the therapist for many years and is now regarded as a coach in modern terminology. A modern world has now demonstrated the flexibility of NLP thinking to solve the puzzle of a variety of environments. Companies around the world are achieving amazing results by introducing NLP thinking into their corporate culture. Athletes from a wide range of disciplines now realize that optimal athletic performance begins in the head. Every week, around the world, people strive for their own personal development, broaden the boundaries of their thinking, and create new opportunities by learning NLP thinking.

What are the advantages of NLP?

NLP is of great benefit to those undergoing treatment as it helps them to quickly stop learning bad behavior and replace it with new, improved behavior. This can have a remarkable effect on a person. Where can you get NLP? For the best results, it is recommended that you receive NLP training from a certified professional. However, there are many NLP books and DVDs on the market today that will teach you the principles of this type of therapy. These can help you learn and apply the NLP techniques yourself. Why do people do NLP? NLP can support all areas of a person's growth and development. NLP itself is not dangerous. However, since this can be learned at home, there is a risk that you will try to address a condition that can be better treated in other ways if you see a qualified psychologist or doctor. Remember that NLP has been used successfully by many, and it is more effective to learn from someone who can teach you properly. Neuro Linguistic programming can be used effectively by individuals to treat a mental illness or to overcome other difficulties. It can also be used by sellers and people who want to influence people. Using the same techniques, sales reps can find out exactly what customers want and help them achieve their goals. Why not see if you can benefit from NLP in your private or professional life? "NLP is an attitude and methodology that leaves a trail of technique." This "attitude" is one of curiosity. So let's take a look at NLP's curiosity. NLP is a tool to understand how the language of our mind creates and executes the patterns we have in life. Yes, but what about modeling? Isn't NLP about "Modeling Excellence" - isn't it just a modeling tool? My answer: Maybe. When we look at the words of NLP - Neuro-Linguistic Programming, we see mind, language, and pattern. We have patterns for EVERYTHING we do - how we learn, fall asleep, be motivated, hesitate, fall in love, eat, exercise, keep a job, get frustrated, be happy, EVERYTHING. And the world of psychology tells us that every thought we have has a chemical reaction; Therefore, each pattern is given a thought (consciously or unconsciously) and a chemical that is produced in the brain. So - a thought and our mind. Of course, NLP is about modeling. We know what we know in this area because we learn from others.

NLP is a tool to understand how the language of our mind creates and executes the patterns we have in life. Once we understand this, we can use a variety of NLP processes to improve, change, or change our thought, behavior, and emotional patterns. When you meet a mother who has problems with her child, try to understand their patterns. What does she say to herself? What emotions does she have? What behaviors? What patterns? When you have a better understanding, then we can apply some of the NLP techniques. For example, suppose your child is prone to tantrums, and the mother has a pattern in which she withdraws from conflict. Perhaps you could help her by changing this pattern so that she is able to face his anger in a supportive and loving way. Try to use a variety of NLP techniques, such as the Swish pattern, partial integration, neurological level alignment, refreshing, erasing emotions, reprinting, etc. The art of NLP is practice - knowing which one processes when to do it. For some people, NLP is a communication tool, a way to negotiate better, a persuasive tool, sales tools, a range of coaching strategies, educational techniques, a modeling tool, natural therapy, and a way of life. Do you know what I'm saying about these answers? They are alright. NLP is all of that, and it's more than all of that.

We are all born with the same basic neurology. Our ability to do anything in life, be it learning a new skill, cooking a meal, or doing business, depends on how we control our nervous system. Therefore, a large part of the NLP is dedicated to learning how to think more effectively and communicate more effectively with yourself and others. Neuro is about your neurological system. NLP is based on the idea that we experience the world through our senses and convert sensory information into conscious and unconscious thought processes. Thought processes activate the neurological system, which influences physiology, emotions, and behavior. Linguistically refers to the way people use language to understand the world, capture and capture experiences, and share those experiences with others. NLP uses linguistics to examine how the words you speak affect your experience.

Programming is strongly based on learning theory and deals with how we code or represent experiences. Your personal programming consists of your inner processes and strategies (thought patterns) that you use to make decisions, solve problems, learn, evaluate, and achieve results. NLP shows people how to re-encode their experiences and organize their internal programming to achieve the desired results. NLP explains how we explain and experience reality using our neurological filters. These filters are programmed in our heads as a result of our cultural and educational upbringing as well as our significant life experiences. Our personal filters (such as beliefs and values) determine how our mind perceives all of our experiences. These perceptions affect our mental and emotional state and lead to related behaviors. So it is our perceptions that determine the quality of every moment of our life. NLP enables us to keep control of our minds by changing our perceptions. When we change our inner maps of reality, we also change our external experience of reality. NLP can be described in different ways. Today you will find NLP applications among trainers and therapists, doctors and nurses, taxi drivers, salespeople, accountants, managers, teachers and animal trainers, workers, parents, and teenagers alike. NLP tells us that the difference between successful and unsuccessful people is not how many resources they have, but how they think, how they speak, and how they act. The way you think is what you create in your inner world. The way you speak and act is expressed in your outside world. If you want to be completely successful, you need to coordinate your thoughts, speeches, and actions.

What is your desired end result? Concentrate on what you want. What is the next smaller achievable step that leads in the direction of your result? Use all of your senses to recognize the signs that confirm that you are on the right track or to warn that you have been redirected. Always try new approaches until you achieve the desired result. Be the person you want to be by getting your result. Some of the areas where NLP is used are Business: coaching, training, negotiation, sales, and leadership development. NLP offers the "how-to-do" for all "what-to-dos" of the other management models. Education: class management; Incorporating the concept of different learning styles: visual, auditory, and kinaesthetic, including values and other deep structural "filters" that affect each person's interest and ability to learn; accelerated learning technologies; Read photo; Spelling and other strategies to improve learning. Therapy: Highly effective short therapy models for the treatment of phobia, trauma, post-traumatic stress, cessation of habits and addiction, allergic reactions, relationship problems, grief, depression, healing of negative emotions, ADD, ADHD, and more. Athletic Performance: NLP is known for its ability to improve golf, tennis, and diving performance. NLP is also widely used to improve the athletic performance of athletes from amateur to world-class.

Both individuals and teams can benefit significantly if they incorporate NLP principles into their training. On the personal side, with NLP: you can enjoy far more control and freedom over your own state of mind, your reactions, and your interactions with others. You will find it much easier to clarify your dreams for the future and identify obstacles that may hold you back. Change the unwanted habits and behaviors that get in your way. Understand the needs and communication styles of your partners and children better. Improve contact and communication with others. See how others use language to influence you. You will find it easier to accomplish your personal and professional goals as you gain better access to your internal resources.

NLP requirements

What do you assume about yourself, others, life, and the opportunities and circumstances of life? Consciously or otherwise, and for the most part, it is unconscious, we have all the things that we accept or assume about life. We don't want that, but we do. These assumptions or NLP requirements can have a profound impact on our lives. When it comes to our targets, hopes, and dreams, we can have recurrent thoughts or feelings that form a psychological barrier between our thinking and our desires, our performance, and even the actions we do or don't do. In matters of the heart, we always have thoughts, beliefs, and attitudes that also influence and inform about how we react to relationships, the opposite sex, and even the sex itself. This internal dialogue then becomes prerequisites that we accept as true regardless of their origin, validity, or relevance, and if they are not radically changed, we hold them in life. So often, this can lead to years passing by and unfulfilled hopes, dreams, and ambitions turning into frustration, regret, or even acceptance of psychological, material, and cumbersome mediocrity. Assumptions or suspected assumptions about anything can serve as protection against possible harm or danger, but if they are illogical, poorly informed, or simply wrong thoughts, they can affect both ourselves and our grasping of the many possibilities that life has for us. A person's presuppositions cannot be communicated directly in what they say, but they are under the surface all the time in their beliefs, attitudes, and even their values. By listening to them, we can learn a lot about their mental world map and how it works. The interesting thing about the prerequisites is that they operate in secret by acting on an unconscious level, and we need to know them on a level to understand what they tell us.

Requirements can have a positive and negative impact on our lives. They can limit us, and they can strengthen us. By assuming that something is or will be what we think it is, both limiting ourselves and our reactions to it, most assumptions are based on what was yesterday, not what is today. Like so many of our beliefs, our assumptions are often just generalizations about the past or what we assumed. For this reason, they are not always objective, as they are the result of a person's unique and individual experience in the world. Because of this, they tend to be subjective and often serve us poorly, which leads to conflicts between our conscious and unconscious desires. For example, a person's life experience may have programmed them on an unconscious level to believe that you cannot trust people. This can lead to conflicts between their conscious and unconscious minds and that they act and behave in a way, or even make decisions that are incompatible with actually trusting someone completely. This can lead to indecisiveness and even strategies in dealing with people that can lead to unrest and even potentially catastrophic consequences. While you may be apprehensive of some of your prerequisites, there will be many that you will only be aware of when they cause conflict, challenge, or even failure or adversity in your life. At this point, such prerequisites can be questioned as ingenious, ineligible, or simply wrong. However, we often need to be aware that our experiences incorrectly reinforce our requirements and cause us to hold onto them through fear, disappointment, or mere justification. The choice is always with us. The choice is always there, but it can only be made if we acknowledge its existence and decide to make positive decisions for our lives. NLP is about realizing that we have a choice AND providing the psychological equipment that makes it the best choice for our lives. The key aspect of all assumptions, or what we call prerequisites in NLP, is their value in strengthening our lives. Regardless of everything, we all inevitably have prerequisites for everything. Take the requirements as the operating system of your internal computer into account. They enable the processing of all other things. Those that fit or fit the operating system go through and reinforce it. Those who don't do so interfere with the operating system by either customizing it or filtering it to stick to it. By taking into account and addressing new and more imaginative or more desirable prerequisites that change remarkably, even a transformation can take place in both thinking and performance. NLP provides a framework of conditions that, although not always empirically correct, can provide a framework for creating positive change.

EXCELLENT SALES WITH NLP TECHNIQUES

We take the meaning out of our experience; that's what NLP is all about. The ability to change the meaning of your products in the eyes of a potential customer is extremely useful for sales professionals. Below are some of the many NLP patterns that can help you with this. NLP-Rapport in a sales environment to increase the responsiveness of your potential customer, NLP-Rapport is really in a sales situation. Using stimulation and guidance, opening anticipation loops, and covert hypnosis are some of the techniques that can increase responsiveness beyond the usual matching and mirroring of your environment. The ability to convert negative feelings into positive motivations would be beneficial in a sales environment. NLP tells us that we can choose how we feel about an event, and there are many NLP tools that can help you with that. You may want to reduce all of your fear of rejection, failure, and low self-esteem and replace it with excitement and confidence in yourself, the product, and your sales process. It may be useful to use these NLP tools for yourself, but consider the options once you've learned to do the same to others, whether it's your sales team or your customers. Every sales professional wants to have the opportunity to make people curious and excited about themselves, their products, and their company. Understanding people with NLP processes one way to make more and better sales is to understand your customers' values, beliefs, and motivations. The basics of NLP are to uncover exactly these things. Behind a person's behavior lies the answer to why they may be buying one product and rejecting another. A good NLP Practitioner course can teach you how to uncover the deepest needs of your customers and how to adapt your product or service to those needs. There are many great uses for hypnotic speech patterns in any influencing situation. The sales department offers one of the best. Once you've gotten rid of all false expectations and the hype, NLP training can give you great insight into the use of hypnotic patterns. Language is just a filter that we use to encrypt the meaning of our experience. The words we use and the way we use them to determine the direction in our minds. If you understand this process, you can direct your prospect's eyes in certain directions. In practice, this means that you can get people excited about things, bypass arguments and objections, and even change beliefs. A simple, hypnotic NLP language technique like future stimulation can eliminate buyer's regrets or bypass costs to focus on results and returns. Hypnotic persuasion tactics are a powerful addition to a sales professional's toolbox. Sales, the perfect NLP context, a good NLP Practitioner course, gives every sales professional a decisive advantage in every area of their lives. For example, we haven't discussed NLP modeling to learn from experts or NLP-accelerated learning skills to quickly assimilate information about your products, competitors, and your market. The question is not whether NLP Sales Professional can help, but whether Sales Professional can survive without NLP techniques.

If you want to learn covert hypnosis, there are a few things to consider. Covert hypnosis is an area that is unique to all other areas of hypnosis. It works by discretely hypnotizing people who are not aware of their consciousness, and therefore they won't notice any suggestions that you put in them. The difficulty with this is that you have to do hypnosis in people so that you don't raise suspicions in them. If you raise suspicions, your suggestions will not work because the person can recognize the suggestions consciously if you want them to be recognized unconsciously. The trick to overcoming this is to make sure that your suggestions are not consciously registered by the person or subject to whom you are doing covert hypnosis. This is easier said than done until you practice, but here are a few things to keep in mind. First of all, you want to make sure that you don't pause when you anchor in a person, change your tonality too much, or give obvious clues as to what you're doing. Instead, let the conversation run naturally and pat the person on the shoulder when you say the word "intimacy" to anchor while continuing the conversation in a completely natural way. This means that the person subconsciously registers that you tap the shoulder with the word "intimacy" without consciously thinking about it. This is an area where many new covert hypnosis practitioners make mistakes, anchor, but obviously do so. Make planting your anchors as discreetly as possible, and you will notice more positive results.

The inner mystery of NLP and how you can easily master your life

NLP is a fascinating topic. Many people think that NLP was created in some kind of laboratory and didn't really exist "out there" in the world. People hear a politician throw out a pattern or two, or maybe use an anchor to suddenly draw the conclusion, "Hey! You must have trained in NLP! What a sneaky bastard!" In fact, NLP was developed by people who are naturally good at persuading and influencing. You see, most people are inherently good at what they do; to some extent, otherwise, they wouldn't. Sure, we have to practice if we want to make a living, but we wouldn't have chosen to do what we do if we weren't halfway decent and liked it. Professional golfers are, of course, good at golfing and enjoy it. Of course, engineers are good at math and enjoy it. Politician? You can, of course, convince and enjoy it. The best just keep doing what works and keep getting better. The truth is that most people who are really good at something don't really know why they are good at it. They only know that they are good at it, and by doing it again and again and measuring their feedback, they get better and better. What makes NLP different is that you take EVERY ability, reverse engineer it, and accept it as your own, "as if" you were a "natural." Very few people have mastered their skills through reverse engineering. But with NLP? Everything is possible. Think about it the next time you see someone who is inherently good at something. The real secret associated with NLP is that you can undo any behavior that someone else has observed and then learn how to do it yourself.

This experience of seeing two people who deal differently with the circumstances and achieve different results tell us something very important about behavior/reactions, and what we actually get for it in life proves the law of cause and effect. Everything has a cause, and how we react to it often determines the effect we experience. So why do fairly rational people who are able to determine the likely results of their behavior seem to be unable to manage that behavior to achieve what they expect from life? Why do we do it anyway, even if we know that our behavior will lead to undesirable results? The answer lies partly in what we have learned unconsciously (experience) and in the internal programming mechanism that causes us to associate results with certain feelings or emotions. As a result, we can often avoid some behaviors that are good for us and seek others that are not in our best interest. Every experience in the brain is interpreted very differently from person to person. We filter, distort, delete, and generalize what we experience through complex mental meshes that selectively sort information and experiences according to pain and pleasure. What we enjoyed before or assume that we will have fun in the future, we filter into the boxes "wanted" or "like to experience again" and filter what we associate with pain in any form (physical, mental or emotional) into the "unwanted" or avoidable box. Because we tend to generalize, erase, and distort experiences and events that have similar components or are in some way comparable, our mind simply categorizes them. It then simply assigns its components in terms of pleasure or pain. All of these associations form factually false memories that create images, sounds, feelings, and sensations in the spirit that we "identify" with these experiences. The result of this filtering and association process can be a dramatic change in our behavior in relation to certain future experiences. What most people just don't understand is that their behavior and reactions are also someone else's external event. Experiences or circumstances, and they become the catalyst that influences others and influences their own unique inner mental processing. For the most part, our entire life experience comes from our relationships with others. Connecting with other people is a basic human need, and through our relationships, we experience ourselves, or at least the effect of ourselves on others. It is the basic process of social education.

While emotions are an important part of human experience, they can negatively impact these relationships if they are no longer imaginative or ineffective. This leads to disagreements, opposites, conflicts and explains the differences that exist between people. The process of filtering is transferred to the hypothalamus, which controls a large part of our functions as an organism. It can make fear the weakest physiological symptoms and arousal the most imaginative drives and impulses. Consider the fear. It is clear that fear (although rare) can be a good and healthy emotion, but what about the most common occasions when it is not? The moment we think of something or associate it with the feeling of fear, the hypothalamus triggers an adrenaline rush in the entire bloodstream, and in a split second, our entire body chemistry is turned upside down. We breathe deeper, and our heart beats faster. Blood pressure rises, and blood sugar levels rise to provide additional energy as the digestive system shuts down and the blood vessels in the skin contract to allow increased blood flow to the muscles; the muscles contract to increase strength. The skin becomes pale, and our eyes widen to give a better view. Wow! All of this due to one thought, and such thoughts often occur without any actual physical threat to the body. We call this "stress." Every emotional state produces biological and physiological reactions in the body, and it is easy to see how this has a fundamental effect on our body, our feelings, our reactions, and consequently also on our behavior. All of this happens in our brains through mere thoughts. Repeatedly enough, the body's response to such thoughts can manifest itself in the form of stress, psychosomatic and nervous disorders, and even illness and death from cardiac arrest or stroke, and even organ damage over time. The biggest challenge for most people is that they only think without being aware of the process that takes place in their brain and body. Most of our responses to life's events are hidden or programmed into us over time, and we just play them off in the mistaken belief that "of just who we are." Few people realize that they have a choice, that they have the right to feel how they actually want to feel, to think the way they want to think. Few people are aware that they can decide how to control their own brain in a resource-efficient manner and how to manipulate their own experiences and results deliberately. Your brain is literally a magic wand, and all you have to do is wave it properly to experience real magic in your life.

CONCLUSION

Everyone longs for success. Each of us has something in which we want to be successful. Most people want to be rich, while others feel that fame gives them the greatest satisfaction. Some consider it the epitome of success to climb the career ladder. Although everyone wants to be successful, some people don't have that kind of experience. This is because most of them give up once they fail. They relax and come to the conclusion that success was not for them. The successful people achieved because they applied the psychology of success. To use it, you have to change your mindset and be able to apply what a particular person calls "the principles of the right character": patience, honesty, punctuality, reliability, and the like. If you want to be successful, you first have to consider these properties that you have to achieve. This is because it is not easy to control and discipline yourself. So you have to train yourself. You should plan first and have a vision. This is after he/she has defined success for him/her. By defining success and knowing where to go, you will be able to stay focused. A person who has no vision cannot be focused because they have not planned what they want to do. One will then write down what needs to be done and then prioritize according to the degree of importance.

"What if you could say goodbye to deferment forever?" Believe it or not, there is a way you can do this! Procrastination no longer has to be your local nemesis. If you try to see it as separate from yourself, you can start to get the upper hand to keep free from the frustration associated with it, but the work doesn't stop there. Eliminate the resistance. If you choose to release it, you must start by eliminating its companion, which is resistance. Much of your hesitant behavior is based on "mental resistance." So it makes sense to find a way to make room for a new way of thinking. How do you fight the resistance? Use affirmations to remove the resistance. Use your words and take measures to achieve this. For example, you could say, "I no longer allow Resistance and Procrastination to rent space in my head and use my mental energy," or "I'm watching Resistance and Procrastination leave me now," or you could take a slightly different approach and say, "I am free to choose postponement and resistance as friends (or maybe as teachers) so that I can learn more about why they held me back and I struggled with them and myself to get things done!" To remove the resistance, you have to be aware of your presence. It's sneaky if you're not careful. Resistance makes your body feel awful. Any reaction you have to a negative feeling is your body's attempt to send you the "red flag" that it is moving. What you may or may not notice is that you can control your "resistance meter," and if you don't want resistance, you can let your mind get over it.

To go one step further, resistance is a by-product of fear. Fear is not that easy to externalize, so we need to broaden the search for answers by looking at the underlying fear that triggered your resistance and caused Procrastination and Resistance to rent space in your head. Determine Your Fear by beginning to wonder when was the last time you felt when resistance led to hesitant behavior. Did you feel anxious, scared, confused, frustrated, angry? Think about it and really try to go deep into the process of your hesitant behavior. First, consider the following three questions: 1. Am I afraid of being rejected by others when I accomplish this goal or task? 2. Am I afraid of not knowing all the answers, so it is better not to take the initiative than to try and fail? 3. Am I afraid to let go of the delay because it has protected me, and if I voluntarily give up something that has become valuable to me, I will not feel lost without it? This should trigger personal introspection if you really want to look for the source of your fear. Remember: "Your fear has led to your resistance that made procrastination possible." It is never easy to look inside and become aware of negative feelings and behaviors. However, if you start this process by letting go of your identity as "A procrastinator," you have taken the first big step to learn how to find your way to success "Externalize, Eliminate and Determine"! However, if you master the basics and are able to put people in a trance, plant suggestions into them, and get the person to respond to those suggestions, you may be wondering what the next step is. Advanced covert hypnosis includes techniques such as instant induction, multichannel hypnosis, instant rapport, and inducing amnesia so that people can never remember an encounter they had with you. These techniques can be hard to master, but of course, if you are at the level you feel ready to tackle, it is, of course, possible to master these techniques. The first technique you should be familiar with is to use pattern interrupts to put someone in a trance immediately. You want to learn how to get someone into this trance just a few moments after you meet them. This is accomplished by creating a reality for the person that the person did not expect. This leads to confusion. Confusion is a common condition we get into every day. If someone says something we didn't expect, if we left something somewhere and then can't find it, or if something else happens that we don't expect, we get confused. This current state of confusion is comparable to a state of trance. Our consciousness receives a number of message units and is overloaded by these message units, which causes this trance state. Because confusion leads to message unit overload, all we have to do is take an action that they find confusing to put someone in a trance.

www.ingramcontent.com/pod-product-compliance
Ingram Content Group UK Ltd.
Pitfield, Milton Keynes, MK11 3LW, UK
UKHW021924190726
13853UKWH00002B/837

9 798201 666019